The
Happy Heart Cookbook
Low Cholesterol Cooking For Life

Also by Harris C. Faigel

The Happy Heart Cookbook (1st Edition)

Alchemy: How Adolescence Changes Children Into Adults

In addition, Dr. Faigel has published more than 100 scientific and research articles in medical journals, including (among others):

- New England Journal of Medicine
- Journal of Pediatrics
- Journal of American College Health
- Journal of the Society for Adolescent Medicine

The
Happy Heart Cookbook
Low Cholesterol Cooking For Life

Second Edition

Revised and Updated

By

Frayda Faigel, MSN
and
Harris Faigel, MD

Rosstrum Publishing
Nashua, NH

Rosstrum Publishing books are available at discount when purchased in bulk for premiums and sales promotions as well as for fundraising or educational use. Based on quantities, special editions can be created to specification. For details, contact the publisher by mail or by e-mail.

An online version of these recipes are available for members of Cook'n. Information is available at NVO.com.

Rosstrum Publishing
8 Strawberry Bank Rd.
Suite 20
Nashua, NH 03062-2763
rosstrumpublishing@gmail.com
www.rosstrumpublishing.com

Library of Congress Control Number: 2013942067

Manufactured in the United States of America
First Printing June, 2013
1 3 5 7 9 10 8 6 4 2

Dedication

This edition of **The Happy Heart Cookbook** is dedicated to all those who need to control their cholesterol and for whom exercise and pills alone are not enough.

The Happy Heart Cookbook:
Low Cholesterol Cooking For Life

Frayda Faigel and **Harris Faigel**

Table of Contents

Introduction

Cholesterol is vital to life, *but* too much cholesterol can block vital arteries and lead to heart attacks and early death.

Where does the cholesterol that causes the trouble come from? It results from a combination of factors, but one of the most important is eating foods high in cholesterol and fat. Changing what you cook and how you cook it makes a difference that can save your life.

Preface

When your doctor tells you your cholesterol or the cholesterol of someone in your family is too high and it has to come down, the information is upsetting and worrisome, but the information should not be confusing or scary. Will it last forever? Yes. Is it contagious? No.

Cholesterol can be too high at any age. Some of us have it because we are overweight or eat the wrong foods. We learned our eating habits when we were children. The response is simple. Lose some weight and adopt sensible eating habits.

Others have inherited genes that make their liver produce too much cholesterol. They need to be careful with what they eat. They will have to exercise. They need medicines.

And some people have both problems. They eat too much cholesterol and fatty food, and they make too much cholesterol as well.

The most important part for everyone to remember is that managing cholesterol is "for the rest of your life."

Low-cholesterol cooking in **The Happy Heart Cookbook** is for the entire family. People who eat too much cholesterol need to eat carefully. People who inherit genes for making too much cholesterol need to eat carefully. Parents with poor eating habits or with bad genes can pass their habits as well as their genes to their children. Those children should be tested and they in turn will have their own children who need to be tested.

The adults who have too much cholesterol or triglyceride in their blood because of their eating habits must eat differently to lower their blood fat levels. They need to start early so their children will develop the food habits and preferences that will protect them when they become adults.

This is a cookbook. It is not a nutrition manual. There are no food value charts or calorie counts. Very few people pay attention or use them even when they *are* included in a cookbook. A person determined to count every calorie and weigh every gram should consult a standard nutrition textbook and then be prepared with a diary, scales and rulers to weigh and measure every morsel.

That is not practical for most people. Therefore, you will only find suggestions in this book.

Chapter I - Understanding Cholesterol

"When diet and exercise alone are not enough, talk to your doctor about . . .." says the ad on TV.

But what kind of diet is that? What can you eat? What should you leave out? And how long does it have to last? Furthermore, there are concerns about the long term effects of the drugs doctors use to lower cholesterol on health and mental function as well as liver or muscles. Therefore, the food you eat, and the way you cook it, is more important than ever.

It has been four decades since cholesterol was identified as a major culprit in heart disease and atherosclerosis (formerly known as hardening of the arteries). It was simple then. A high cholesterol level was connected with early heart attacks. Diet could help.

The years since have made the story more complex. Researchers isolated a long list of chemicals called lipoproteins that carry cholesterol in the blood. Light-weight lipoproteins, called low-density lipoproteins or LDL carry cholesterol to the cells where it is needed to manufacture and maintain cell walls and for storing cholesterol in cells. Heavier lipoproteins (HDLs) carry excess cholesterol away from the cells for elimination from the body. HDL is a good lipoprotein because it limits the amount of cholesterol while LDL is the bad guy making it build up. So, too much cholesterol and LDL are clearly bad for you and a lot of HDL is good. The proportion or ratio of HDL to the total cholesterol in the blood measures the risk of early heart disease. The lower the ratio of HDL to the total amount of cholesterol, the better.

In the beginning, cholesterol, and the fats the body used to make it, were the only targets of treatment available and controlling what you eat was the only way to get cholesterol down. Today we know that only one-fourth of the cholesterol in the blood comes from food. The rest is made in the liver. You can reduce your cholesterol about ten percent simply by changing what you eat.

The cholesterol made in the liver can also reflect what you eat since certain fats increase the amount the liver makes. Unfortunately, the rest come from your genes. If one or both of your parents had a liver that made too much cholesterol or not enough HDL, you could have the problem, too.

Aerobic exercise, exercise that makes you sweaty and short of breath and increases your heart rate, can also lower cholesterol, about another five to ten percent.

The first medicines used to treat high cholesterol interfered with its absorption. They cut cholesterol both from the liver and from what you eat. They worked, but unfortunately, they were not as successful as hoped for. They are still used today as a part of total care, but no longer are considered the only way to manage cholesterol.

Fiber in your food can absorb some of the cholesterol. Eating more fiber in foods like vegetables, oats and other grains does help, but it is not enough by itself.

Scientists have learned how to interfere with making cholesterol in the liver. They developed medicines to increase the production of HDL and limit that of LDL. The medications are called statins and they change the chemical processes in the liver. They also affect those same chemical processes in muscle cells and, in some people, can therefore cause aches and pains in the arms and legs even while they are protecting the muscle in the heart.

For a long time, doctors have known that alcoholics might die of liver disease, even though they had healthy arteries.

Alcohol does seem to limit cholesterol from building up in arteries so moderate use of alcohol can be acceptable. Wine contains resveratrol, thought to be a chemical that lowers cholesterol, but resveratrol pills have not been effective.

Obesity can increase cholesterol and LDL. Diabetes can too. Weight loss and the careful management of diabetes, along with vigorous aerobic exercise can lower cholesterol, can lower LDL, can raise HDL and can reduce the risk of a heart attack. Unfortunately, it can be hard to include those routines in a frantic life coping with the demands of work, home and family. There always seems to be reason not to go to the gym, always an excuse to eat less healthy foods, always a justification for a little higher blood sugar

Surgeons have improved gastric surgery during the last 35 years and have added the Lap-Band to their treatments. Most people with very severe obesity do lose weight and lower their cholesterol after the surgery, and the majority of them keep the weight off. However, some learn how to eat multiple small high-calorie meals and gain the weight back. When stomach surgery works, cholesterol falls and for those with diabetes, that disease gets better, too. A change in eating habits is an essential part of this surgery, as is a commitment to follow your doctor's instructions.

Changing what you eat was the first way to control your cholesterol and it remains a mainstay of treatment. And so, 40 years after the first edition of **The Happy Heart Cookbook**, it is back with a new revised and updated edition to help you control your cholesterol and your LDL, reduce your risk of an early heart attack, and maybe even help with your weight and diabetes as well. Just remember, improvement requires that you do it for the rest of your life.

Heart Attacks: How Early Is Early

Physicians recognized 200 years ago that arteries blocked by hard deposits in their walls could cause death. However, heart attacks were rare before the 1890s when reports of men dying from them began to appear in medical journals. No one understood the causes of the plugged arteries then, and most of those men were sixty years old or more when they died.

Heart attacks became more common in the 1930s and 1940s. Men were victims of those attacks far more often than women.

By the 1950s, doctors understood that hardened, fatty deposits in the arteries of the heart caused blockages that resulted in heart attacks. An early heart attack then was still thought to be one before the age of sixty.

As the twentieth century ended, more heart attacks began to occur in younger men and women in their forties and even thirties. Today, an early heart attack is considered one before fifty and women are as affected as men.

Doctors now understand the need to look for family histories of early heart attacks, test for abnormal cholesterol and LDL and signs of hardening arteries and begin treatment, all before age forty. However, not every family knows it has a history of early heart attacks and family history is not enough of a guideline for tests. By 2005, the national standard for first tests of cholesterol, regardless of family history, was 21. In 2011, the American Academy of Pediatrics recommended first tests by age twelve, before puberty.

Earlier And Earlier

At first, it was never clear why fatty streaks appeared in young soldiers in the 1890s, showed up as fatty deposits in the doughboys of World War One and worsened in the GIs of World War Two. Then cholesterol was identified in those deposits, which led to an examination of the food people eat.

Diets began to change in the 1840s when railroads and refrigeration made it easier, faster and cheaper to transport food long distances. Whereas vegetables and grains made up much of earlier diets, meats and poultry became more common. And where working men got the lion's share of the meats in earlier times, women and children have gained more access.

Most babies were breast-fed in the 1860s. By the 1890s, nearly one in three newborns was bottle fed. By the 1920s, nearly half were never fed at the breast.

Commercial food companies began to sell prepared baby foods in the 1930s. Before the 1920s, babies rarely started on solid food until they were nine months old.

Today it is clear that cows' milk and solids fed early will stress a baby's kidneys that are not ready for the chemicals in prepared foods, and those foods can add to the risk of developing early fatty streaks in the arteries.

The change to cows' milk and the early feeding of solid foods set the stage. Better availability of a greater variety of foods, more access to meat and other foods high in fat and cholesterol, and more of them at younger ages increased the burden and risk of rising cholesterol and early heart attacks.

In the 1950s, fast food stores erupted on the scene. Hamburgers and cheeseburgers, fried chicken, bacon and doughnuts became the four "basic" food groups for Americans looking for a fast way to get food without having to prepare it. By the 1980s, fast food had become the bane of life for doctors trying to deal with obesity, diabetes and early heart disease.

There is another factor. When Americans did manual labor on farms and in factories, they got a lot of aerobic exercise that helped burn the foods they ate and limited the amount of cholesterol they absorbed. It kept them slimmer, too. Today, few men or women do that kind of manual labor. Machines have taken on much of the hard work. Clerical, store and office jobs have limited the rest.

The decrease in exercise and the changes in eating habits have magnified the problems. Early fatty deposits now start in infancy, obesity begins in childhood, and the problem continues throughout life.

Careful studies by doctors and life insurance companies showed that too high a cholesterol level and plugged arteries in the heart can give you a two-, three- or even four-fold increase (over people with normal cholesterol levels) in the chance of having a heart attack before age 60. Other research has shown you cannot wait for your first heart attack to take care of your heart. You have to do it throughout your life.

Cholesterol is important in your body. Like other fats, it is a building block for cell walls. It is also a basic chemical the body uses to make stress and sex hormones. Fats can be saturated, with hydrogen filling every available space on the carbon atoms, unsaturated with very little hydrogen attached, or partially saturated with a smidge more hydrogen. Saturated fats increase cholesterol levels; unsaturated fats can lower them.

Cholesterol is not the only villain. Cholesterol is just one of many fats in your foods that affect the risk of an early heart attack. Doctors recognize several kinds of bad fats, some from what you eat and some from what your body makes.

In the ordinary American family, almost half of total daily calories come from fat and most of those are saturated. On the other hand, in an Asian family, only 30 percent of calories come from fats, and only 20 per cent are saturated. Americans have more heart attacks than Asians.

We all need cholesterol to stay healthy, but too much over a lifetime can make us ill. What you eat and how you prepare it can make a big difference in your health, the quality of your life, and how long you live. It is a program that needs to start in infancy and last a lifetime. It is a program that can make a lifetime last longer.

Good Fat Bad Fat

Some of the fats you eat can be really bad for you. Those are animal fats that are found in fatty cuts of beef and pork, the fats in poultry and the fat in butter and buttery cheeses and other dairy foods. They include both natural and man-made saturated fats, fats that have hydrogen attached to all of their carbon atoms. They are the building blocks the liver uses to make cholesterol. Many foods that contain a lot of saturated fats offer a double whammy because they also contain a lot of cholesterol.

On the other hand, most liquid vegetable oils are unsaturated, mono-unsaturated or polyunsaturated. They have only a little hydrogen attached to their carbon atoms. They do not contain cholesterol or contribute to cholesterol production. These include olive oil, peanut oil, canola oil, grape seed oil and corn oil and all of those are good to use in salads and cooking.

Palm oil is the one vegetable oil that is not good for you. It is notorious for raising cholesterol and should not be included in what you eat or cook.

Margarines are made by partially saturating liquid fats. In the past, most contained both saturated and unsaturated fat, but manufacturers have learned how to avoid that.

Margarines now are partially saturated and most contain neither cholesterol nor fully saturated fat. There is another kind of fat that you need to avoid. These are the trans fats the commercial food companies now try to avoid and that the food labels now identify. Nearly all trans fats in the food supply are a kind of partially saturated fat that occur during food production. Eating trans fats lowers HDLs and raises LDLs, thus increasing the risk of a heart attack. A different kind of trans fat exists in beef and pork and paradoxically can lower LDL and raise HDL. Pay attention to the trans fat information on the label of a commercially prepared food product and you will do well.

When the first edition of *The Happy Heart Cookbook* was written, eggs were an enemy because cholesterol in the yolks needed to be avoided. Since then, researchers have shown that omega-3 fatty acids in eggs can balance the cholesterol and can make a limited number of eggs per week a reasonable choice. Otherwise, the earlier advice to use liquid egg substitutes is still important.

In the past, pork was also a problem because of its fats. During the interval since then, pork producers have raised pigs with less total fat, and less harmful fats as well, so that now, pork loin roasts are leaner and can be part of a low cholesterol eating plan.

In general, a reasonable rule of thumb requires that you eliminate trans fats, limit solid fats and rely on liquid ones for food and cooking. It is true that it is nearly impossible to entirely avoid saturated fats and cholesterol in what you eat. Nevertheless, you can keep them to a minimum and still eat well.

Free Of Fat Or Sugar

It is a strange conundrum that during the last two decades, people have been getting fatter while they have been able to buy and use more and more foods that are lower in calories, sugars and fats.

People who use calorie-free sodas do not lose weight. They eat more food.

People who use sugar substitutes do not lose weight or lower their cholesterol level.

People who eat salads for lunch do not lose much weight either. They use more high-calorie salad dressings.

People who try to eat little or no fat do not lose weight. They make up the calories elsewhere.

People who go to Weight Watchers or get their meals from companies like Jenny Craig or Nutrasystem or attend support groups like Overeaters Anonymous might lose a little weight, even as much as ten percent or more from where they started, but two years later most have gained the weight back.

There are two problems. For some, taking away calories in one form lets people replace those calories in another way. There is no overall control or change in what they eat. Their total calories never change. Neither does their weight.

For others, supervision from an employee or member of [1]Weight Watchers® or Overeaters Anonymous®, for example, or buying food from Jenny Craig® or Nutrasystem®, for example, turns the responsibility for a new life style over to another person. When the supervisor is gone, when the prepared foods are done, there may be no internal controls in place to take over. Most of these people return to their old habits and their original weight. And they go back to their original cholesterol levels too.

Food supplements, protein supplements, omega-3 oil supplements, even vitamin supplements have not been shown to have many long term benefits in controlling cholesterol.

High protein diets can help. Vegetarian diets can help. High fat diets can help. Low fat diets can too - for a while but, sooner or later, South Beach, North Beach, East Beach or West, Mediterranean or Asian, none of them makes a lasting impression because they do not last for most people. High carb, low carb, no carb or sugar free, everyone craves the tastes of family and childhood. Everyone returns to the familiar. And everyone risks returning to the problems those foods create.

Party Times

Parties of every kind are a challenge for people who need to control what they eat. That includes parties in restaurants, someone else's home and parties during holidays. Although you might not think of vacations or travel as party times, consider what you eat in the restaurants while you are on your way. Tailgate parties for a fall football game, hotdogs and burgers at the baseball park, picnics in a meadow or a vineyard all present a challenge to anyone who needs to control cholesterol.

---

[1] Names of companies are used for illustration only and do not represent approval from, nor recommendation for any group or company. Names are the trademarks of each individual company or entity.

Look at these events as a brief respite from all that daily control. They are treats that let you make a change for a meal or two. They let you off the reservation for a day. And then you go back to your regular routine. The keys in this paragraph are: **brief**, **a meal** and **a day**.

Have one hotdog, not two or three. Leave some of that burger behind. Have one beer and then drink water. Have small 'thank-you' helpings at the dinner table. Take doggy bags at restaurants even if you will never use the food in them. Be a member of the dirty plate club.

Yes, there really is a dirty plate club. It is the club for all of us who were child philanthropists cleaning our overstuffed plates, eating because our mothers reminded us of all the starving children somewhere else in the world. None of us ever asked how eating less or too much here helped or hurt starving kids there. We just cleaned our plates. Now we have to change that habit and leave food behind.

Use smaller plates whenever you can. A little food on a small plate fools the eye and then the mind into thinking there is more than there is. Start with a bowl of soup or a salad before the meal to begin filling your stomach and let you feel full sooner. Eat slowly so your sense of fullness can catch up with the amount you are eating. And no second helpings - ever.

Keep the alcohol under control. Although red wine is considered helpful in lowering LDL and raising HDL, the calories in those drinks count, and they can count a lot.

Diet Is A Problem

There is serious trouble with using the word 'diet.' A diet can be what you eat every day. But a diet is also something you might use to control your weight, your blood sugar or your cholesterol. The first kind of diet is everyday food and never changes much. The second kind is temporary, something you start and stop when you achieve whatever goal you set. Or, more often unfortunately, when you fail and give up because it does not work.

You are often urged to eat a 'balanced diet,' but you may not know what that is. Government agencies try to help with food pyramids or sample plates that change every few years and are hard to track. They never tell you what to eat or how to figure out if your own eating pattern is 'balanced.' Nearly every one of those advises balance at every meal, or at least every day, but that is not really necessary. Scientists know that the body averages what you eat over a 30 day cycle for most foods, for a six month cycle for a few others. Half of all the proteins, carbohydrates, minerals and vitamins B and C dissolve in water and what you eat today will still be in your body four to six weeks later. If you miss a little of this or that today, your body will do the averaging and you will be okay. Problems only happen when you make a habit of missing something important, like iron or iodine. Half of fats and vitamins A, D and E that dissolve in fat, last six months or more. The hard part is making changes that will last a lifetime. It takes dedicated unhealthy eating for several months to get deficient in one of these.

Since the first edition of **The Happy Heart Cookbook**, fast food outlets have multiplied. Many of their menu items have grown in size, calories and fat. Although they do offer some items like salads, the dressings have a lot of calories. It may be reasonable to eat there once or twice a month, but doing it more often is not a good habit to develop.

When **The Happy Heart Cookbook** first appeared, Julia Child was the only chef on television and she became a celebrity. Other chefs made names for themselves in magazines, and then appeared on TV. Today there is an entire TV channel dedicated to celebrity chefs and cooking competitions. That is creating a new list of celebrity chefs. For all of that, their recipes are hard to follow on TV even when they are available on computer, and many are too complex for most home cooks. Few home kitchens regularly stock parchment paper, butcher string or even the variety of pots and utensils and ovens and stoves and electrical appliances that appear on the television cooking shows. Their best contribution has been to improve cooking techniques and knife skills.

There were a few cookbooks available forty years ago. None considered the problems of obesity, diabetes or high cholesterol. Today, a new cookbook with a special focus is published every week. Nevertheless, obesity, diabetes and high cholesterol play a very small part in any of the new ones during the year.

The Happy Heart Cookbook

These are the basic rules for having a healthy heart:
- Be consistent.
- Eat a broad range of foods.
- Keep fats and cholesterol in your diet as low as you can.
- Pay attention to exercise.
- Work with your doctor.
- Make it last your entire lifetime.

Fat increases the feeling of satisfaction and fullness. You need a little bit.

Put desserts in a small glass cup. You don't need a lot.

There are no dietary supplements that burn fat.

"Light" foods do not reduce total daily calories.

The Happy Heart Cookbook gives you great recipes to help you with sensible eating. It is for people who already have a problem with high cholesterol, but the recipes are equally important for families and for those who want to avoid having a cholesterol problem.

This book is full of ideas and recipes to help you keep your cholesterol under control. It is written to keep you healthy and your heart happy.

In this book, diet is eating for a lifetime. This is forever. This is a new way to cook and serve food and eat that can help you manage your cholesterol, keep the good stuff high, the bad stuff low and the total fully controlled.

Eat well!

Chapter II - Fads, Foods And Diets

Many people vaguely remember just enough nutrition information from school health classes to mix with superstition, fear, television ads, internet information and misinformation, faith-healing and high-pressure sales tactics promoting all kinds of food fads. Fortunately, most of those become boring very quickly and rarely last long enough to cause permanent harm.

On the other hand, some food fads that do last can be damaging. People, particularly children, have died of malnutrition, not because they did not have enough food to eat, but because they were reaching the end of a fad diet that was promoted as a cure for a laundry list of physical, emotional and social ills. Regardless of whether you drink a gallon of water a day, take laxatives or enemas to "cleanse" your system or consume a bushel of carrots or grapefruit a week, none of these truly improves health, nutrition or resistance to illness or early heart disease. In fact, they could be dangerous for some people.

There have been chocolate bar diets, fat diets, alcohol diets, hot dog diets, egg diets, fried food diets, mayonnaise diets, fruit diets, calories-don't-count diets – you name it and someone made money promoting it. Careful testing shows none of these has long-lasting beneficial effects.

'Health' food and 'natural' or 'organic' foods and 'free range' and 'grass fed' and fed-only-vegetables-or-flower-petals have become big business. Some 'health' foods are made without the preservatives that are added commercially to prolong shelf-life, and 'natural' or 'organic' foods are grown without fertilizers or other chemicals. Careful studies have shown they are no more nutritious than other foods at the market.

Fiber

Fiber can absorb some of the cholesterol and fat in what you eat and help to lower the amount you absorb. The fats and fatty acids stick to the fiber and are carried through the intestine to be eliminated at the other end so they cannot get into your bloodstream.

Oats, whole wheat and wheat grains, leafy vegetables and many fruits are excellent sources of fiber that can also help digestion and normal bowel function. That is the reason that oats, whole wheat and vegetables like broccoli, chard, lettuce, cabbages and squashes should play a large role in your eating plan.

A high fiber breakfast includes these high fiber cereals or grains and make up one of the servings you need each day. After that, you need three more servings that can include a salad and a serving of vegetables with dinner and fruit like an apple, a pear or grapes or plums or dried fruit for dessert or a snack. Be sure you get enough of these so that you keep your fiber level up and your cholesterol under control.

Omega-3 Fatty Acids

Omega-3 fatty acids are chemicals that you need for health, but your body cannot make them, so you have to get them in foods that contain them, like salmon, tuna and halibut, sardines, anchovies, bluefish, trout, mackerel and herring or seafood from krill or algae as well as nuts. The omega-3 fatty acids reduce inflammation that contributes to chronic diseases like heart disease, so increasing your servings of these fishes, fresh or canned, caught or farm raised to increase your level of omega-3s is a very good thing to do.

Unfortunately, most Americans eat too many foods that are high in omega-6 fatty acids that can cause inflammation, and not enough that contain omega-3s that reduce it. The omega-3s in fish and fish oil and in walnuts reduce the risk of heart attack and stroke. They are good for people with high levels of cholesterol and triglycerides because they raise HDL levels and reduce those of triglycerides. Studies have shown that eating at least two servings of fish per week can lower those heart attack and stroke risks. The Mediterranean diet is particularly good because it emphasizes foods high in omega-3. People who follow that diet have a lower risk of heart disease because they have higher HDL and lower triglyceride levels.

Fish, fish oils and nut oils like walnuts are the main source of omega-3 in what you eat. You should eat at least two meals of these each week. Omega-3 also found in flaxseed, canola, soybean and pumpkinseed oils. These are good sources of omega-3, but fish is still the best.

Always try to get your omega-3 from the foods you eat, not from supplements. Twenty years ago, the information available suggested that omega-3 pills might help. Today, the newest data show that the benefits from omega-3 pills and supplements are very small and the dollar costs are very big. The pills provide only minimal protection and they are not a good substitute for real food. So eat your fish and vegetables instead.

Additives

Prolonging shelf-life is an advantage to the shopkeeper who can keep the product in the store longer, increasing the chances of selling it. Prolonged shelf-life can help the homemaker by reducing both waste and trips to the market. The very few people who think they are sensitive to these additives should not make that diagnosis themselves, but should rely on the tests of well-trained physicians to track down the problem.

'Natural' Foods

Plants make no distinction about whether identical chemicals come from the compost heap or the fertilizer maker – as long as the chemicals themselves are the same. All fertilizers are chemicals, whether they come from factories or farm waste. If the 'trace elements' some believe are found in nature are truly important, then there should be nutritional differences between genetically identical plants – garden type identical twins – raised in the same place under the same conditions, but with different fertilizers. There are none.

Local and hothouse produce can taste differently from that raised a thousand miles away because the latter ripen in the truck on the way to market while the locally grown vegetables ripen on the vine or the plant. Some have a different flavor because they are not genetic twins. As long as the fertilizer provides the plant what it needs to grow and prosper, the plant cannot suffer a deficiency disease to pass on to you.

Health And Food

Food and nutrition research has not shown that 'health foods' or 'natural foods' are better for you than other good, fresh, high quality foods. The benefits of 'health' or 'natural' or 'organic' foods are more likely to be psychological than pharmacological.

Don't be fooled by glib, self-assured pitchmen out to make a bundle by selling you snake oil. Physicians who care for adolescents have shown that young people are taller, heavier and mature physically earlier than their parents because of the quality and variety of what they eat. That could not happen if their food lacked nutrients they need to grow.

Vitamins

Vitamin fads are worth mentioning because they can victimize people in their pocketbooks and because they help to keep other food myths alive. Vitamins are necessary for health. That is clear. But vitamin supplements may not be.

Vitamins A, D, E and K are fat soluble. That means they dissolve in fat and are stored in the fat in the body. Diseases from a lack of these develop slowly. It can take the average adult three years of a totally deficient diet to become ill from a lack of one of these. Very young children are much more sensitive because they are growing rapidly and can develop a deficiency while still toddlers.

Vitamin A is important for vision and Vitamin D for bone health, growth and healing. Vitamins A and D are added to so many manufactured foods that any adult eating a broad range of dairy products is likely to get enough of them. The problem is getting adults to do that.

Lactaid pills can make it easier to use milk, cheese and other dairy products. Soy milk and almond milk can often substitute for cow's milk.

Infants under the age of one drinking prepared formulas are as well supplied as are older children who drink milk because nearly all milks have these vitamins added to them. Vitamin D works with calcium to build and keep bones strong. Adults, particularly women, who drink no milk and consume very little cheese, yogurt or other dairy products can develop a calcium deficiency and osteoporosis, a weakening of their bones that will make them prone to fractures when they get older. Fortunately, your body will manufacture Vitamin D when you expose your skin to sunshine and Vitamin D deficiencies are uncommon in adults. On the other hand, children today who do not consume calcium or who are slathered with so much sunscreen that they do not produce enough Vitamin D have become victims of rickets, a disease that disappeared several generations ago.

Vitamin K is made for us by the normal bacteria in our intestines and is important in forming blood clots when we have a cut. We don't have to worry about not having enough unless we are given very powerful antibiotics that wipe out those bacteria and stop the supply.

Vitamin E deficiency only occurs in very small newly born premature babies, infants born too soon to get enough across the placenta from their mothers before birth.

The B vitamins and vitamin C dissolve in water and don't last as long in the body. Still, it usually takes about three months with a total lack of one of them before deficiency symptoms begin. Breads, grains and cereals along with meats are good sources of the B vitamins. When you see the word 'enriched' on a package of flour, bread, cake or cookies, it means the normal B vitamin content that might have been diluted or removed during milling has been restored.

Vitamin C is in so many fruits, vegetables and vitamin enriched fruit drinks that it can be hard to avoid this vitamin. It would take very dedicated eating today for most of us to develop scurvy from a vitamin C deficiency.

Very young children who do not yet eat a broad range of table foods, ill or elderly people on very restricted diets, and the very poor who eat unbalanced diets do risk getting a Vitamin B or C deficiency unless they change their diets or supplement them with extra vitamins.

Sixty years ago a famous biochemist theorized that high doses of vitamin C would protect him from the common cold or make his colds shorter. Researchers tested that idea and found that he was wrong. Unfortunately, his ideas made front page headlines while the overwhelming data showing he was wrong were buried in the back. Vitamin C is still promoted as a cure or preventer for colds and a source of quick energy, despite science that says otherwise.

Vitamins are not a source of energy. They are chemicals our bodies need to be able to process the foods we eat. If you are short of vitamins, you are probably short of a lot of other foods and minerals you need, too. A vitamin supplement might correct that for you temporarily, but you have to change your eating habits to make it last.

Vitamin Overdose

Few people know that there are vitamin poisoning diseases from too much of a good thing. Too much vitamin A can cause headaches, skin rashes and increased pressure inside the skull. Vitamin D is necessary for good bone health in the right amount, but too much causes tender painful bones. Vitamin C in large doses can cause crystals in the urine that burn during voiding and can collect as stones in the kidneys.

Antioxidants

For many years, antioxidants were promoted as important for health. The idea was that oxidizing chemicals in the body were harmful for your health and foods that had a lot of antioxidants in them would be good for you. Millions are made promoting blueberries, acai berries and a lot of other foods. There is no science behind these promotions - merely an idea, one that made a lot of money for the people selling it.

However, the idea is wrong. Oxidants are important when you mobilize your immune system to fight an infection. Antioxidants can reduce the amount of oxidants and interfere with a quick recovery. Scientists now know that increasing the amount of antioxidants in your food is not particularly helpful and too much can actually be bad for you.

Low Cholesterol And Fads

Is a low cholesterol diet one more fad? No, it is not. It is based on sound scientific evidence accumulated over the last forty or more years. It stresses eating a wide range of foods in a well-balanced eating plan. It demands that you limit one kind of food and replace the calories, not with another that has magical qualities, but with many others that are just less harmful.

A word about corn oil. As good as it is, corn oil is not the least saturated oil in the market. Safflower oil and sunflower oil are less saturated, but they can cost more. Corn oil margarines are easier to find and those made from less saturated oils are often not worth the extra cost. You get more benefit from switching from butter, lard or shortening to corn oil than you would by switching from corn oil to safflower or sunflower seed oils.

And another word about olive oil. It is a neutral oil that does not raise cholesterol and is the oil of choice in the Mediterranean. It can add flavor to any recipe and should be part of any balanced eating plan.

So, you see, while the foods you eat at each meal are important, your body will do an excellent job of averaging what you eat over a full month's time. That is why having 'something special' once a month can neither help nor hurt you. It is consistency and faithfulness to eating a low cholesterol diet and to eating well that are important and will let you last your whole life.

Chapter III - Reading Nutrition Labels

Demanded by the government, every food package has nutritional information on it. The label begins by telling you how large a standard serving is in both grams and household measure. Next, it tells you the total servings in the container and the calories in each one. Be careful. The calories are per serving, not per container. If a container says "ONLY 100 calories per serving, but the container has 2.5 servings, that would give you 250 calories if you eat the entire container.

The food types – fat, protein and carbohydrates – are listed next with the amount in each serving and the total recommended in a balanced 2000 calorie day. The label tells the amount of saturated fats, unsaturated fats, cholesterol and salt (sodium) and, perhaps, other minerals as well. If you are modifying what you eat to lower cholesterol, you need to be very familiar with those labels.

A low cholesterol diet is low in total daily fats. It keeps calories from fat at about 30 percent of the total, so it is important to select foods that are low in both cholesterol and fat. It is also important to choose foods that are high in polyunsaturated fats or to be sure there are more of them than saturated ones. Many foods have two, three and even four times the polyunsaturated fats as saturated and these are better than when the proportion is the other way round.

The other part of the label you need to read is the list of ingredients. They are listed in a particular order, beginning with the most common one and ending with the least. If fat is one of the first items listed, it is one of the commonest parts of the food.

The problem common to most people is limiting portions to the serving size marked on the label. Portion control is not part of the way most people measure their meals. It needs to change.

Low Cholesterol Eating

Look for key words on labels. It is not enough for food to have little or no cholesterol. Other fats are important.

The process of hardening liquid vegetable oils calls for adding hydrogen, called hydrogenation. It makes them saturated. Vegetable shortening is hardened vegetable oil. These products are low on the totem pole of choice.

Lard is animal fat. However, it is unique because, unlike other fats, it can raise HDL (the good stuff) and lower LDL (the bad guy) a little. It has another benefit in frying because the smoking temperature is higher so you can fry at higher temperatures and the food will absorb less fat when you do, but you still need to limit the amount you use. Beef fat, butter and butterfat are also animal fats. You can be sure that they are high in saturated fats and should not be on your dinner table.

Low cholesterol eating requires you to substitute low fat, low trans fat and low cholesterol ingredients for ones that are higher in saturated fats and cholesterol. It asks you to choose foods that are naturally low in fat, saturated fat and cholesterol. And it means you pay attention to all of it for the rest of your life.

Cooking Oils

All vegetable oils are not alike. Some vegetables, like coconuts and palm kernels, contain oils that raise cholesterol and must be avoided. Others, like corn and safflower and sunflower seed oils can help a low cholesterol diet. It is not enough to know that a food contains vegetable oils, even ones that manufacturers like to label 'pure' (Isn't that silly? Is there any manufacturer using impure ingredients and advertising that?) You need to know the *kind* of oil being used.

Read labels carefully. Pay attention to the size and number of servings in the package as well as the nutrients. Don't be fooled by labels that say 'Cholesterol Free' in large letters on the front and then list saturated fats as important ingredients on the back. We know of several products that do that.

Finally, ask your doctor, a certified nutritionist or registered dietitian about anything you do not understand. Once you learn to get the most from what you read and read the labels all the time, it's easy.

Chapter IV - Cooking Principles

Eat foods low in cholesterol as well as those that are low in total fat and saturated fats. Animals differ in the amount of fat and cholesterol in their meat and those meats have different amounts of fat in different parts of the animal. Poultry, veal and fish have less total fat that beef or pork. There is less fat and cholesterol today even in beef and pork because ranchers and farmers have learned to raise leaner animals. Organ meats like liver and fatty tissue like bacon have more fat than other meat does. Sausages, delicatessen meats and luncheon meats usually have a lot of fat and cholesterol too.

Meat from the front of a cow, like the shoulders, is lower in fat and cholesterol than meat from the loin and there is more fat in prime cuts than in choice and even less in select. Learn the names used for those cuts where you live because the words can be different on the East and West coasts. Choose the ones that are better for you

Frying

With all the fat and cholesterol naturally present in foods, there isn't any reason to add more. That's what frying can do, especially frying in saturated fats or frying at low temperatures. People with high cholesterol levels should not eat foods fried in saturated fat.

Foods can absorb the oils and fats they are fried in. Meats seared on the outside can seal in fat that might otherwise ooze out. Potatoes need to be baked, boiled or mashed. Fish should be broiled, poached or baked.

People with high cholesterol should broil, bake, braise, roast or slow-cook their meats because even lean meat contains fat. Keep it moist by basting with stock, bouillon, broth or wine instead of drippings. If you prepare a stew or soup stock, make it a day ahead, chill it and skim off the hardened fat. If a recipe calls for browning meat first, you can do it on a rack under the broiler. Some foods can be 'fried' in a nonstick pan using an anti-stick spray.

Some foods want to be fried. Use a polyunsaturated oil, a low-cholesterol margarine or a neutral oil like olive or peanut oil.

Balancing Beef, Pork, Fish And Poultry

Fish and poultry are lower in fat than beef and pork. They should be the main course in four or five meals a week. Veal is desirable too, but nowadays it can cost so much that we hate to recommend it.

The fish with the lowest fat are cod, turbot, haddock, flounder, ocean perch, brook trout, tilapia, sea bass and red snapper. The fattier fish are mackerel, salmon, tuna, whitefish, bluefish and lake trout, and all of those are lower in fat that beef, pork or poultry. Eat fish two to three times a week.

Poached fish produces a meal lowest in fat. Poach in white wine or a broth of water, onions and herbs. Don't boil fish. Cook it only till it flakes.

Poultry has its own problem. There is a lot of saturated fat in the skin, some in the dark meat and less in the white. Remove the skin from poultry and stick to the white meat. It is better to remove the skin before cooking since the meat can absorb some of the fats, but even removing the skin after cooking and before eating is a help.

Ground Meat

Ordinary supermarket hamburger is twenty to thirty percent fat by weight, has a lot of cholesterol and about 60 percent of its calories come from fat. Lean ground beef in those markets is ten to fifteen percent fat, about 40 percent of its calories comes from fat, and it provides less cholesterol. The careful eater does not consume much regular supermarket hamburger, but buys extra-lean beef or grinds it himself.

Ground pork, chicken and turkey at the supermarket can be surprisingly high in fat and cholesterol. Ground pork often includes the trimmings after pork chops and roasts are prepared for sale. It has a lot of fat in it. Ground chicken and turkey are usually made from parts of the bird that do not sell well or that are removed when the meat is being packaged by the butchery. That means that there can be a predominance of dark meat and a lot of skin and fat mixed in with the ground poultry, increasing both the fat and cholesterol content in what you buy.

Invest in your own meat grinder. Use lean cuts of beef and pork and trim off the visible fat. Remove the skin and fat from chicken and turkey and balance legs and thighs with breast meat. Make sure there is fish and skinless poultry on your plate often. And pay attention to how you cook that food every day.

Other Foods

Many recipes call for cheese. Low fat Parmesan and sapsago cheese go a long way as substitutes for more saturated products. A sprinkling of grated Romano cheese can add flavor without a lot of fat or cholesterol.

Cooked vegetables taste better when lightly steamed with lemon juice, herbs and spices. Rosemary, oregano, basil, thyme, garlic, chives, pepper, dill, mint, sage, tarragon and marjoram add zest and interest. Other spices include caraway, bay leaf, chili pepper, cilantro, cinnamon, cloves, coriander, mustard and nutmeg. Start with ¼ teaspoon and then let your taste be your guide.

Even though mayonnaise is made from whole eggs, you can use it because one egg is made to absorb a full cup of polyunsaturated oil. If you use it sparingly, the actual amount of cholesterol you will eat will be small. And you can make your own mayonnaise in a food processor with a liquid egg substitute to be certain the oil really is polyunsaturated and is better than other alternatives.

Use dried packaged salad dressings. Add your own olive oil and vinegar instead of using the commercial liquid dressings.

You can separate eggs or use packaged egg whites or liquid egg substitutes instead of whole eggs for your cooking. Make gravies with bouillon or stock instead of pan drippings. Prepare poultry stuffing in a pan, not inside the bird where it can absorb fat. Use pretzels instead of potato chips, tuna in water instead of in oil, marshmallows instead of other candy, Canadian bacon in place of fried bacon and baked apples instead of apple pie.

Making Changes

The previous edition of **The Happy Heart Cookbook** had an entire chapter of charts and lists showing foods to substitute for others because there were very few alternatives then. Since then, food makers and grocery markets have provided an enormous selection of very good alternatives and *Eat This, Not That* is the new version of substitutions in print and on television. You do have to read the nutrition labels to find the substitutes, but they are there.

Here are other things you can do to make your recipes taste better even while you keep the fat and cholesterol down.

Make soups richer by using skim milk, but adding a small amount of flour and polyunsaturated margarine. Replace a square of baking chocolate with three tablespoons of cocoa together with a tablespoon of polyunsaturated margarine. Make your own pies and pie crusts because bakers often use hydrogenated and saturated fats in their products. Master the recipes in this book for pastry, graham cracker and corn flake crusts.

Make fruit pies in a deep casserole to reduce the amount of crust in proportion to the filling. With twice the filling of an ordinary pie, each serving has fewer calories, fats and cholesterol.

Flash frozen fish has become available everywhere. You can use it in place of fresh fish all the time, and it may even be less costly than the fresh varieties. Even towns and cities far from the oceans now have access to seafood. Be careful the fish does not thaw on the way home. Treat it the way you would ice cream to keep it from developing crystals and an odd flavor of iodine.

Chicken casseroles need white meat instead of dark. Tuna casseroles are a good alternative. Beef casseroles made from lean cuts of meat make good substitutes for fattier chops or steaks and benefit from a lower cost than these pricier cuts.

In recent years, new grains like farro and quinoa and new pastas like Israeli couscous have become popular. So have yams and sweet potatoes. They make good changes from dishes made with potatoes or rice.

You can substitute desserts of fruit for cakes or cookies. You can substitute homemade salad dressings for the bottled kind. You can use nonfat milk instead of whole milk, although you may need to make that change gradually by moving first to 2% milk and then to 1% milk before going the whole way.

Poultry

If you really have to fry chicken, skin it, dip it in a wash of a liquid egg substitute mixed with a little Dijon mustard to make the coating stick to the bird, and then roll it in crushed grape nuts, crushed corn flakes or puffed rice, flavored bread crumbs or panko before sautéing in a small amount of polyunsaturated oil or with a small amount of one of the anti-stick sprays in a nonstick pan. You can make your own bread crumbs from hard stale bread with a grater or a food processor.

Turkey is more versatile than simply the bird on a holiday table. Without the skin, smoked turkey slices make super sandwiches. Turkey breast cut into slender cutlets and then pounded thinly can take the place of veal in every recipe. Turkey breast or turkey roll can be a wonderful main course any time of the year. Left-over meat can be sliced for sandwiches or diced for turkey salad.

Meats

Lean beef means flank steak, shoulder roasts and the round. Sirloin and tenderloin are fattier. Veal can be trimmed well, as can veal sirloin. The leanest part of lamb is the leg, the fattiest the ribs and the loin.

Pork producers have reduced the amount of fat in pigs. Carefully trimmed and prepared, pork tenderloin, ham, loin roasts and chops can be used. Canadian bacon can substitute for the fattier American type and can even be substituted for ham in casseroles.

At one time, imported Danish and Polish hams had less fat than domestic ones and were preferred for low cholesterol eating. However, the American pork industry answered the challenge. It merely requires careful shopping to find what you want.

Meat gravies made from the drippings of roasts have been staples on dinner tables everywhere. Substitutes can be made by draining the fats from the pan, scraping up the loose brown particles from the bottom, mixing in polyunsaturated margarine and heating them together over low heat for 10 minutes. Use stocks, broths or bouillon cubes and water to extend your gravies if you need a little extra.

Vegetables And Fruits

Vegetables have no cholesterol and they are an important part of your menu. Combine two vegetables with nuts such as slivered almonds, cashews, pine nuts or chopped pecans or walnuts to add new flavor and variety to your dinner table. Steam fruits and vegetables until they are just tender, but crunchy, to retain their vitamins and minerals.

Salads can be low in calories as well as in cholesterol. The vegetables should always be fresh and crisp. Dressings should be made with polyunsaturated oil and added to the salad just before serving so the leafy vegetables will not wilt.

Mayonnaise is made with whole eggs, but average only five milligrams of cholesterol in a teaspoon. It is not enough to worry about if you only use a small amount in your dressings.

Raisins, dried plums, cranberries, blueberries or fresh diced fruits added to vegetable salads completely change their character.

Milk

Nonfat dry milk powder is whole milk with the water and fat removed. It may not always behave like whole milk in your recipes so you will want to make some adjustments. The usual way to improve the milk is to liquefy a quart of milk according to the directions on the package and then add an extra ⅓ to ½ cup of the dry milk powder.

To reconstitute instant nonfat dry milk from the powder for drinking, follow the directions on the package carefully and then refrigerate it for 12 hours before you drink it. Some packages of instant nonfat dry milk contain individual envelopes that each make one quart. If you find this milk too watery, use five envelopes instead of four to make one gallon. This changes the consistency, makes it feel more like whole milk in your mouth, and increases the protein by 20 percent. Finally, this milk can be whipped and stabilized so it will not be runny.

Coffee whiteners are a problem. Most are made from palm or coconut oil and cannot be used by the cholesterol-conscious person. Choose the cholesterol-free whiteners to use in beverages, over fruit or in any way you would use coffee cream.

Pasta

Egg noodles are made with flour and eggs. These contain a little cholesterol and you do need to consider that if you are limiting the number of eggs you eat.

On the other hand, macaroni, couscous and other pastas have fewer eggs and are generally free of cholesterol. Use them as often as you want.

Menus

Planning a low cholesterol menu means limiting the number of meals of steaks, prime rib or other fatty meats. It means using more fish and poultry. Meats and poultry should be roasted on a spit or a rack so that the fat can drip off into a catch pan.

Home ice cream makers let you make ices, sherbets, frozen custards, frozen yogurts and even iced milk without including cholesterol. Use egg whites, gelatin and polyunsaturated margarine and stir constantly during freezing to prevent crystals from forming in the dessert.

Chapter V - Substitutions

Do you have a favorite recipe? Does your family have a favorite dish? Now that you are cooking low cholesterol meals, can you keep on using them? Of course you can.

It will take some changes and some experimenting, but everyone can make substitutions. Use polyunsaturated margarine in place of butter or shortening in your cooking and baking. Occasionally you may want an extra buttery flavor. Add a few drops of liquid imitation butter flavor to do it.

Many products made with vegetable oils do not label which oil is used. Sometimes it can be palm or coconut oil because those are vegetable sources. They are not the kind you want in a low-cholesterol kitchen. Find others.

Chocolate comes from cacao, a vegetable, but it has a lot of fat that is almost fully saturated. You can use cocoa in its place, substituting polyunsaturated margarine for the fat in chocolate. Although most chocolate bars contain cocoa butter and need to be limited, some candy is made with cocoa and liquid vegetable oils. Read the label.

Eggs

Every large egg contains 275 milligrams of cholesterol. Ordinarily, people eat between 1500 and 2000 milligrams of cholesterol a day, but a diet low in cholesterol only allows 300. One egg is pretty much an entire day's allotment. Using egg whites or commercial egg substitutes works well. Follow the instructions on the container and use the equivalent of one egg for each whole egg in the recipe.

Some recipes call for a lot of eggs and the outcome may not taste right if you use egg whites or an egg substitute. Use one whole egg for every fourth substitute 'egg' to improve the flavor. Remember that the cholesterol in a whole egg is in the yolk. There are many recipes where the whites of two eggs can do the work of one whole egg.

But in the world of low cholesterol cooking, what can you do with those leftover yolks? If there is a member of the family who does not have to limit cholesterol, use the extra yolks in egg salads or special treats for them. If not, you might be stuck feeding them to the family pet.

Carbohydrates

People who have too much triglyceride in their blood as well as too much cholesterol have to be careful with the amount of carbohydrates they eat. Carbohydrates are sugars and starches. You can keep starches down by limiting candy, breads, cakes and baked goods. Like a diabetic, you can use sugar substitutes in place of sugar as a sweetener, foods with a higher glycemic index and whole wheat products instead of bleached flour.

What about 'dietetic' foods? If your doctor wants you to reduce carbohydrates along with exercise and medication, you may want to consider these. However, you have to read labels very carefully since some do contain too much fat or cholesterol. Don't be fooled by a label that reads 'Dietetic.'

Other Foods

Many recipes that call for beef or veal can be made with turkey. With care, they can have the same flavors and less cholesterol.

Replace whole milk with the fat-free skim milk kind. It may take a while to get used to the different taste and feel in your mouth, but once you do, you might wonder how you ever drank that other stuff at all.

Breads are generally low in fats, but some are made entirely without fats. Choose those when you can.

Water ices and sherbets and frozen yogurts are made with low cholesterol ingredients whereas ice cream can contain as much as 15 percent butterfat and some have even more.

Fruits and gelatin make good desserts. There are many recipes available on the Internet that make wonderful treats using them.

Chapter VI - Eating Out

Restaurant food is a problem for people on low cholesterol eating plans. Restaurants use a lot of butter and few low cholesterol fats. A lot of frying is done in butter or oils that are saturated, and much restaurant food is fried.

The best restaurants use prime meats. These are the most marbled meats and have the most fat and cholesterol. The other problem is that the menus rely heavily on beef, along with recipes that include cream and cheese sauces. These have even more fat. Even restaurant brown gravy contains an overwhelming amount of animal fat.

Less expensive restaurants and fast food outlets do even more frying and the hamburgers they serve are about 30 percent fat by weight and 60 percent of the daily calories in each serving. Many still prepare French fries in saturated fats.

Still, eating out is fun for everyone, and it's a necessity for some. Short of carrying your own food in a paper bag and having a picnic, there are some things that you can do.

Start every lunch or dinner with a salad. Work in those fish meals (stick to the fish species with scales, of course). Eat more poultry or pastas. Ask for margarine or olive oil in place of butter. Have baked potatoes and use margarine on them. Bacon-flavored soy protein bits can add flavor when they are available.

Stick to oil and vinegar salad dressing on the side and dip your veggies in the dressing instead of pouring the dressing over them. The creamy dressings contain too much fat. Spruce up a salad with a lemon wedge.

Appetizers should be soup, fruit salad or vegetable juice. Herring is excellent, and an occasional shrimp cocktail is acceptable, but the liver pate is not.

Cooked vegetables are low in fat until the chef prepares them in a butter or cream sauce. Ask for olive oil and lemon juice instead.

Beverages present another issue. Few restaurants serve nonfat milk, but most do have cocoa made with skim milk. Ask for it. Coffee and tea are never a problem by themselves, but become a problem only when you put cream in them. And alcohol should be limited because of the calories and, for those on a low carbohydrate diet, because alcohol is one more carb.

Desserts. Well, if you want one, stick to fruit, gelatin or sherbets. You can bet that cheeses, pastries and the other menu goodies can be too rich for your blood.

Chinese Cooking

Chinese restaurants are a special case. Most food there is made with lots of vegetables and they are stir-fried in a little peanut oil. Chinese food is generally a good choice. Just remember to stick to the fish, poultry and noodle dishes.

Eating Out Italian

Pizzas consist of bread, some tomato sauce and cheese. Some are also made with a little olive oil. They are fine nutritionally, but watch out for the toppings. Vegetables are great, but meatballs, pepperoni, sausage, bacon and extra cheese make those pizzas high in cholesterol and saturated fat. Submarine sandwiches (also known as gyros or hoagies) made with meatballs or cold cuts are often high in those fats you do not want to eat. Stick to a sandwich filled with tuna or chicken or turkey and vegetables.

Lunch

Which brings us to lunch. The safest thing to do is bring your own, but it is not always convenient. Treat large lunches in restaurants like dinners. Order a soup, a salad or a light fish dish or pasta. Whenever possible, order from the luncheon menu (smaller portions) and leave the dinner entrees alone.

For lunch in a sandwich shop, choose the tuna salad, the chicken or turkey. Remember that cold cuts are just big fat overweight sausages as are hot dogs. They all have too much fat. The deli meats, like pastrami, corned beef, spiced ham and roast beef, taste good, but contain too much fat, even if you ask for a lean cut.

If you eat a lot of lunches in restaurants, this can be a real problem. If you eat there once in a while, you can adjust what you order and live with it.

Lastly, when you are a guest in someone's home, don't worry. You won't be struck down with a heart attack on the spot for eating the food that is served. Accept small portions, carefully remove all the visible fat and politely decline second helpings. And if the dessert is one of the rich gooey kinds, refuse it gently with the comment, "My doctor has me on a very strict diet," or request some fruit for the same reason.

Speedy Eateries

Let's talk about the fast food franchises for a minute. The meat is usually commercial grade beef and, surprisingly, could be lower in fat than the hamburger you buy at your supermarket. Most franchises offer a choice between a plain burger and one that is doused in a 'secret' sauce. Cheeseburgers and fishburgers come with the same kind of sauce. Some serve ham or chicken and nearly all now have salads and lower calorie choices. The problem with the chicken is that it is fried. The trouble with the salad is that the dressing has a lot of calories and even fats.

If you do eat in one of these emporiums, order a small plain hamburger, a plain fish fillet or ham, all without cheese or the special sauce. Go to places that broil; it's better for you.

Some of the milk shakes are made with iced milk. Those are okay. The rest have too much butterfat and cholesterol.

The fried chicken is greasy and the spices are in the skin and the coating. That's where the flavor is and that's why you have to lick your fingers. The chicken is probably acceptable, but you have to remove the batter and the skin and some of the flavor (the reason you are eating there in the first place).

Party Time

Special events come up so often in everyone's life that keeping to a low cholesterol eating plan all the time is difficult. The problems really accentuate between Thanksgiving and New Years when traditional recipes and constant parties are everywhere. Birthdays, anniversaries, christenings, confirmations, graduations, weddings, Bat and Bar Mitzvahs challenge every diet. Special religious times like Lent and Passover make their own demands when you are trying to keep fats and cholesterol and saturated fats under control.

Many of the solutions in this book apply here. When eating at home, make careful substitutions in favorite recipes. Use low cholesterol and polyunsaturated oil when cooking. In restaurants, make choices carefully. Eat part and take the rest home for lunch another day. At another's home, take small portions and avoid second helpings. Eat the pretzels, nuts and popcorn at parties and leave the chips and dips for the other people. If possible, choose the unsalted snacks.

Have desserts without the ice cream topping. Leave the whipped cream and a small sample of the dessert on the plate.

And then, once a year, reward yourself. Ignore all the rules and eat whatever you want. After that day is over, go back on the plan for another year. Do it once a year and it will never hurt you, and it certainly makes life and eating more interesting and fun.

Chapter VII - Commercially Prepared Foods

Many commercially prepared foods are made with ingredients and recipes that permit them to be part of a low cholesterol eating plan, but don't be fooled by labels that read 'Diet' or even ones that list the amount of cholesterol or trans fats in them. The cholesterol may be low, but if the product is made with saturated fats, you have to leave that out of your foods anyway.

If you have any doubts about a product, consult with a trained nutritionist or a registered dietitian. The dietary department of your local hospital or the nutrition department of your state university can give you the information you need.

Delicatessen

Variety adds spice to life and a spicy smelling delicatessen in your neighborhood is a delightful asset. Unfortunately, a lot of deli meats will not help you lower your cholesterol.

Let's look at deli or 'luncheon' meats. Salamis and bologna are basically like sausages with an obesity condition and the problem with *all* sausages from hot dogs to pepperoni is fat. There is too much fat and too much cholesterol in all of them, even the ones that 'Answer to a higher authority.' The same is true of spicy prepared meats like pastrami, spiced beef and corned beef (unless you can get really lean corned beef). Except for the occasional treat, you need to limit how often and how much of them you eat.

You may be able to have corned beef at home. Buy a ready-to-cook first cut corned beef brisket and trim it of every bit of visible fat before you cook it. Then get the rest of the fat off afterwards as you slice it to get the fat down to more acceptable levels. The meat slicers and the sandwich makers at the deli don't take that much care.

Sliced roast beef and ham should also be homemade and trimmed of every speck of visible fat. If you absolutely must buy meats at the deli, buy large pieces, take them home and trim and slice them yourself.

One of the best things about meats at the deli is the super thin slices. Buy a meat slicer of your own. Home slicers are available and serviceable restaurant slicers can be had from restaurant suppliers. Never use a slicer without a hand guard or it might be part of *your* hand in your next sandwich.

What else is there at the deli? The smoked turkey, sliced turkey and sliced chicken breast are lower in fat. The dried meat products are also good substitutes for the fatty kinds.

You already know that fish with scales are low in fats and cholesterol, and that's pretty much all the fish at the deli. Smoked salmon, carp, sable and whitefish, although they are 'fatty' fish, are excellent substitutes for the deli meats.

Cole slaw is made with mayonnaise, but there is so little in a serving that the fat or cholesterol is negligible. Potato and macaroni salads contain more, so you may want to make those at home instead.

Finally, many older people have high blood pressure as well as high cholesterol and while this is not a low-sodium cookbook, we want to add a note about that. Salt is a real hazard to people with high blood pressure and many foods in the deli counter besides the pickles and pickled foods are made with a lot of salt. All the herring, sausages and spiced meats have too much salt for a person on a low salt diet. That leaves the chicken and turkey breast and the smoked Nova salmon. It's not a bad selection, and it's certainly better than nothing at all.

Chapter VIII - Eat For Life

There is no diet in **The Happy Heart Cookbook**. Diets are short term eating plans people use for special purposes. There are diets for people with diabetes, for people with kidney disease or gluten sensitivity or food allergies or intestinal problems. There are diets for gout and liver disease and for stomach ulcers and for other intestinal disorders. They all are for a current problem. None have been promoted for life. None have given consistent advice for a person who needs to control cholesterol forever. On the other hand, every recipe in **The Happy Heart Cookbook** can be adapted to meet the needs of any of those medical conditions.

Here are some sample ideas for meals that use the recipes in **The Happy Heart Cookbook** and will help make cholesterol less of an enemy and more a simple item in daily nutrition.

Breakfasts

SAMPLE A:
    4 ounces fruit juice or ½ cup fresh fruit
    1 egg poached or boiled or 1 cup liquid egg substitute, scrambled or in an omelet
    1 slice whole wheat toast
    1 small turkey sausage (optional)
    ½ tomato, grilled
    2 mushrooms, grilled

8 ounces nonfat milk
Coffee or tea

SAMPLE B:
4 ounces fruit juice or ½ cup fresh fruit
1 cup dry cereal or oatmeal
8 ounces nonfat milk
Coffee or tea

SAMPLE C:
4 ounces fruit juice or ½ cup fresh fruit
3 4-inch pancakes
2 tablespoons pure maple syrup
8 ounces nonfat milk
Coffee or tea

SAMPLE D:
4 ounces fruit juice or ½ cup fresh fruit
2 4-inch by 4-inch waffles
¼ cup fresh or frozen berries
2 tablespoons pure maple syrup
8 ounces nonfat milk
Coffee or tea

Note: Scrambled eggs, fried eggs and omelets should be prepared in nonstick pans using a nonstick spray.

Lunch

SAMPLE A:
1 cup soup
½ sandwich
1 apple, pear, peach, apricot or small bunch of grapes
8 ounces nonfat milk
Coffee or tea

SAMPLE B:
   1 cup fresh vegetable salad
   2 ounces chicken, turkey or lean roast beef
   2 tablespoons vinaigrette salad dressing
   1 slice toast
   1 teaspoon margarine for the toast
   8 ounces nonfat milk
   Coffee or tea

SAMPLE C:
   4 ounces of poached or grilled salmon
   1 cup fresh salad
   1 cup fresh fruit or fruit salad
   8 ounces nonfat milk
   Coffee or tea

SAMPLE D:
   1 slice pizza with mushrooms
   1 apple, pear, peach, plum or apricot or a small bunch
of grapes
   8 ounces nonfat milk
   Coffee or tea

Dinner

SAMPLE A:
   4 ounces fresh fish, shrimp or scallops, poached or
grilled
   ½ potato, boiled, grilled or mashed
   2 tablespoons low fat sour cream or cottage cheese
   1 cup fresh vegetable salad
   2 tablespoons vinaigrette salad dressing
   1 cup cooked vegetables
   Juice of ½ lemon
   1 cup fresh fruit salad
   8 ounces nonfat milk

Coffee or tea

SAMPLE B:
    6 ounces steak, pork, chicken or turkey
    ½ potato, boiled, grilled or mashed
    2 tablespoons low fat sour cream or cottage cheese
    1 cup fresh vegetable salad
    2 tablespoons vinaigrette salad dressing
    1 cup cooked spinach, broccoli, squash, cabbage
    Juice of ½ lemon
    1 cup fresh fruit salad
    8 ounces nonfat milk
    Coffee or tea

SAMPLE C:
    3 ounces dry pasta, cooked for 8-9 minutes
    3 ounces tomato sauce or pesto
    1 tablespoon grated Parmesan cheese
    1 cup fresh vegetable salad
    2 tablespoons vinaigrette salad dressing
    ½ cup ice cream
    Coffee or tea

SAMPLE D:
    1 cup soup
    1½ cups macaroni and cheese
    1 cup fresh vegetable salad
    2 tablespoons vinaigrette salad dressing
    1 cup fresh fruit salad
    8 ounces nonfat milk
    Coffee or tea

Snacks

If breakfast is very early, a snack in the middle of the morning with coffee can increase energy and get you through to a noon lunch. If dinner will be late, a small snack or pre-dinner appetizer will lower your hunger and let you eat a smaller, healthier dinner.

Fruit, a 100-calorie fiber energy bar, an 8-ounce serving of nonfat milk, or four home-made peanut butter cracker sandwiches will work in the morning. A small apple, pear or plum, a 2-ounce serving of cheese with 3 or 4 crackers, or another serving of peanut butter crackers can get you through until dinner an hour or two later.

Freezing grapes makes a good way to change the taste and texture, to have just one at a time, and to eat just a few as a snack.

Once a month, skip all of this, treat yourself, indulge your whims and enjoy your freedom to eat it all. And then go back to the eating plan every day, every meal till the next time.

Chapter IX - Appetizers

Vegetables And Dips

Chill fresh raw vegetables like carrots, radishes, broccoli flowerets, celery and green, red or yellow peppers and cut into slices or sticks for low-fat appetizers. Thin sticks of turnip, zucchini, yellow squash, asparagus spears, endive leaves, fennel, Chinese cabbage or cauliflower work really well.

~~

Avocado Cheese Dip

1 cup low fat cottage cheese
¼ cup nonfat milk
1 ripe avocado
2 tablespoons lemon juice
½ teaspoon kosher salt
⅛ teaspoon Worcestershire sauce
¼ teaspoon Tabasco sauce (optional)
¼ cup minced green onion or chives

Beat the cottage cheese and milk till smooth. Halve the avocado, remove the seed, scoop out the pulp and mash until smooth. Combine the mashed avocado with the rest of the ingredients and mix until smooth and thoroughly blended.

~~

White Bean Dip

1 can cannelloni beans, drained
3 cloves garlic
½ teaspoon cayenne
2 tablespoons extra virgin olive oil

In a blender, puree the ingredients until smooth. Chill before serving.

FRAYDA FAIGEL AND HARRIS FAIGEL

Spicy Black Bean Dip

1 pint plain low fat cottage cheese
1 10½-ounce can condensed black bean soup
1 teaspoon minced onion flakes
¼ teaspoon garlic powder
⅛ teaspoon Tabasco sauce

In a blender, mix the ingredients together until smooth.
Chill before serving.

~~

Caviar Dip

2 slices white bread
1 cup water
Juice of 1½ lemons
1 small red onion, finely chopped
½ cup polyunsaturated oil
5 ounces carp roe caviar

Trim the crusts from the bread and soak the bread in the
water. Squeeze the water from the bread and blend at a
medium speed with the lemon juice and onion till smooth.
With the blender running, add the oil in a slow thin stream.
Stir in the carp roe. Chill before serving.

~~

Clam Dip

1½ cups low fat cottage cheese
½ cup nonfat milk
1 7½-ounce can minced clams, drained
½ teaspoon chopped chives or green onion
1 teaspoon chopped flat leaf parsley
½ teaspoon kosher salt
1 clove garlic, finely chopped
¼ teaspoon black pepper, freshly ground

Whip the cottage cheese and milk together in a blender.
Fold in the remaining ingredients well with a spatula. Chill
before serving.

Cottage Cheese Dip

8 ounces low fat cottage cheese
⅔ cup mayonnaise
⅓ cup ketchup
2 teaspoons horseradish
¼ teaspoon Worcestershire sauce
1 garlic clove, finely chopped
¼ teaspoon sage
¼ teaspoon kosher salt
1 tablespoon chopped parsley

In a blender, mix the cottage cheese, mayonnaise and ketchup till smooth. Mix in the remaining ingredients. Chill before serving.

~~

Mongolian Yogurt Dip

8 ounces plain low fat Greek yogurt
1 package dehydrated green pea soup mix
¼ cup chili sauce

In a blender, mix the ingredients until smooth. Chill before serving.

~~

Creamy Garlic Dip

1½ cups mashed potatoes
8 garlic cloves
¼ cup extra virgin olive oil
1 tablespoon fresh lemon juice
1½ teaspoons kosher salt
¼ teaspoon freshly ground black pepper
¼ cup low fat chicken stock

Peel, crush and mince the garlic finely and mash it in a large bowl. Add the mashed potatoes and mix with a fork. Beat in the olive oil slowly until fully absorbed. Mix in the lemon juice, salt and pepper. Add the chicken stock in a slow stream and blend until smooth and creamy. Chill before serving.

Eggplant Dip

3 medium eggplant, peeled and cut into ¼ inch thick slices
½ teaspoon polyunsaturated oil
3 tablespoons extra virgin olive oil
½ pint tzatziki
1 tablespoon fresh lemon juice
1 garlic clove, crushed
2 tablespoons flat leaf parsley, finely chopped
¼ teaspoon kosher salt

Lightly oil a flat cookie sheet, lay the eggplant slices on it in a single layer. Coat the slices with oil and then turn them over. Broil the slices for 15 to 20 minutes until soft and slightly browned.

When the eggplant is cool, squeeze out the bitter juice and then blend until smooth in a blender or food processor. Add the olive oil slowly while blending until smooth. Add the tzatziki and mix in thoroughly. Mix in the remaining ingredients. Chill before serving.

~~

Hummus (Garbanzo Bean Dip)

1 can chickpeas (garbanzo beans), drained, liquid reserved
3 tablespoons fresh lemon juice
4 garlic cloves
¼ cup tahini (sesame seed paste)
¼ teaspoon kosher salt
1 tablespoon extra virgin olive oil
1 teaspoon paprika
1 tablespoon flat leaf parsley, finely chopped

In a food processor, combine the chickpeas, lemon juice, cloves, tahini and olive oil into a creamy paste. Blend in the salt. If the paste is too thick, slowly add some of the reserved chickpea liquid until the paste is the consistency of mayonnaise. Chill and garnish with paprika and parsley before serving with wedges of pita bread.

Onion Soup Dip

1 cup low fat plain yogurt
1 cup low fat cottage cheese
1 package dry onion soup mix
¼ teaspoon dry chili powder

In a blender, combine the yogurt and cottage cheese until smooth. Stir in the onion soup mix and chili powder. Chill before serving.

~~

Caponata

1 large eggplant, peeled and cut into ½ inch cubes
2 large celery stalks cut into ½ inch pieces
1 6-ounce can tomato paste
3 tablespoons sliced green olives
3 tablespoons sliced black olives
3 tablespoons capers
1 teaspoon kosher salt
⅓ cup vinegar
4 tablespoons extra virgin olive oil

In a large pot, heat the oil at a medium-high setting and sauté the eggplant until soft.

Add the celery and sauté until beginning to soften (7-10 minutes). Add the tomato paste, olives and capers, mix well, reduce the heat and simmer for 10 minutes. Add the salt and vinegar and simmer for 2-3 minutes more.

Cool, pour into a storage container and chill
Serve with crackers or pita bread triangles

~~

Dipping Oil For Bread

1 cup extra virgin olive oil
1 teaspoon red pepper flakes
3 cloves garlic, finely minced
½ teaspoon rosemary

Combine the oil and spices in a jar, cover and refrigerate overnight. Return to room temperature before serving.

Hors D'oeuvres

Stuffed Mushrooms

1 pound fresh brown or white mushroom caps, wiped and dried
½ pound ground turkey
3 tablespoons breadcrumbs
1 egg, beaten
1 tablespoon minced onion
1 teaspoon minced garlic
½ teaspoon kosher salt
¼ teaspoon freshly ground black pepper
Soy sauce

Mix the ground turkey, breadcrumbs, egg and spices until fully combined. Stuff the mushroom caps with the mixture. Place the mushrooms with the stuffing side up in a baking dish and brush with soy sauce. Bake at 350 degrees for 30 minutes. Serve hot.

~~

Artichoke Bits

1 15-ounce can artichoke hearts, drained and cut in half
¼ cup extra virgin olive oil
¼ cup red wine vinegar
1 teaspoon minced garlic
1 teaspoon Dijon mustard
6 ounces dried beef jerky, softened in bouillon and cut into ½ inch strips

In a blender, combine the olive oil, vinegar, garlic and mustard until smooth. Marinate the artichokes in this dressing for four hours. Wrap each artichoke piece in a strip of jerky and secure with a toothpick. Bake on parchment paper on a cookie sheet at 300 degrees for 10 minutes.

Sardine Canapé

2 cans of Brisling sardines
1 tablespoon minced red onion
1 teaspoon mayonnaise
Cucumber slices, red pepper, or endive leaves

Carefully remove the bones from the sardines and mash with a fork or in a bowl until smooth. Combine with the onion and mayonnaise. Chill and serve on cucumber slices, spears of sweet red peppers or in endive leaves.

~~

Gravlax

1 pound salmon fillet
1 bunch fresh dill
½ cup sugar
¼ cup kosher salt
1 ounce vodka
1 tablespoon capers
1 tablespoon red onion, finely chopped.

Carefully remove all the small bones from the salmon.
Place a layer of ½ of the fresh dill in the bottom of a 4 inch by 9 inch glass baking dish.
Mix the sugar and salt together and spread over the dill. Place the salmon, skin side down, on the dill. Spread the remaining fresh dill over the salmon.
Place a layer of clear plastic wrap over the salmon and weight it down with a large can of tomatoes, for instance. Pour the vodka into the baking dish. Cover the container with plastic wrap and refrigerate for one week.
Remove the salmon from the container, wash off the dill and liquid thoroughly and wrap in clear plastic wrap. Refrigerate for 3 more days. Unwrap the salmon and slice on an angle very thinly.
Serve on crackers or rye bread with capers and chopped red onion.

FRAYDA FAIGEL AND HARRIS FAIGEL

Tuna Pâté

1 cup plain low fat yogurt
2 tablespoons chili sauce
2 tablespoons chopped parsley
2 teaspoons dry onion flakes
½ teaspoon Tabasco sauce
3 cans tuna in water, drained and flaked
Stuffed green olives
Crackers or celery

In a blender, combine the yogurt, chili sauce, parsley, onion and Tabasco. Stir in the tuna gradually and mix until thoroughly blended. Pack the mixture into a small bowl, cover with clear wrap and refrigerate for 3 hours. Remove the wrap. Hold a platter over the top of the bowl and invert the bowl to unmold the pâté. Garnish with green olives and serve with celery or crackers.

~~

Personal Size Pizza

6 whole wheat English muffins or whole wheat pita bread if desired
½ cup extra virgin olive oil
8 ounces marinara sauce
1 6-ounce skim milk fresh mozzarella cheese ball, cut into 12 slices
½ cup grated Parmesan cheese

Split the muffins into top and bottom halves and place with the cut side up on a cookie sheet lined with parchment paper or aluminum foil. Drizzle each half with olive oil. Spread the marinara sauce on each half and spread each first with a slice of mozzarella and then sprinkle with Parmesan cheese. Broil until the cheese melts.

Eggplant, mushrooms, onions, green peppers or hot peppers may be added.

Use whole wheat pita bread for thinner crust pizzas.

Herring Salad

8 ounces herring tidbits in wine sauce
1 Granny Smith apple, peeled and cored
1 small boiled potato
¼ cup cucumber pickle relish
1 hardboiled egg white
½ teaspoon sugar
¼ teaspoon freshly ground black pepper
Celery stalks, sweet mini-peppers or endive leaves

Chop and combine all ingredients. Chill. Serve on endive or celery stalks or stuff into sweet mini-peppers.

~~

Marinated Mushrooms

1 cup white vinegar
2 tablespoons extra virgin olive oil
½ teaspoon minced garlic
½ teaspoon dry oregano
½ teaspoon dry thyme
½ teaspoon kosher salt
½ teaspoon fresh minced parsley
1 pound white mushroom caps, wiped and dried

Combine the vinegar, oil and spices and mix well. Add the mushrooms and refrigerate for at least 3 days, stirring occasionally. To serve, drain the mushrooms and serve with toothpicks.

~~

Chevred Celery

6 ounces goat cheese
¼ cup golden raisins
2 tablespoons honey
2 tablespoons pine nuts
4 celery ribs cut into 3-inch pieces

Combine the goat cheese, raisins, honey and pine nuts in a bowl. Spoon the mixture into the hollows of the celery. Refrigerate and serve cold.

FRAYDA FAIGEL AND HARRIS FAIGEL

Honey Glazed Lamb Meatballs

Meatballs
2 teaspoons polyunsaturated oil
1 onion, finely diced
2 cloves garlic, finely diced
¾ cup plain bread crumbs
¾ cup vegetable stock
2 pounds ground lamb
½ cup liquid egg substitute
1 teaspoon dried rosemary
1 teaspoon dried sage
1 teaspoon dried oregano
10 drops Tabasco sauce
½ teaspoon kosher salt
½ teaspoon freshly ground black pepper
glaze
2 teaspoons polyunsaturated oil
1 medium onion, finely diced
½ cup honey
½ cup cider vinegar
1½ cups apple cider

Meatballs
Warm 2 teaspoons of polyunsaturated oil in a small pan over medium heat. Add the onion and garlic and sauté until soft.

Mix the bread crumbs and vegetable stock in a bowl and let sit until the bread crumbs soften. Thoroughly blend in the onion, garlic, lamb, egg substitute, rosemary, sage, oregano, Tabasco, salt and pepper. Use a small ice cream scoop to shape the mixture into small balls, place them on baking sheets covered with parchment paper and bake at 400 degrees for 25 minutes.

Glaze
Heat 2 teaspoons of polyunsaturated oil in a skillet over medium heat. Add the onion and sauté until soft and golden. Stir in the honey, vinegar and cider, bring the mixture to a boil and simmer for 20 minutes until the glaze is reduced in half.

Add the meatballs to the glaze, mix well to thoroughly coat them, transfer to a serving dish and pierce each with a toothpick for service.

~~

Smoked Salmon Canapé

1 pound farmer cheese
¼ cup nonfat milk
1 teaspoon horseradish
1 pound smoked salmon or gravlax, thinly sliced
12 baby bagels cut in half
Black olives, sliced

In a blender, whip the farmer cheese, horseradish and milk until smooth. Spread each bagel half with the cheese mixture, top with strips of salmon and garnish with black olives.

~~

Oriental Chicken Wings

48 chicken wing drumsticks, skinned
1 teaspoon garlic powder
½ cup water
1 16-ounce jar of grape jelly
1 14-ounce bottle of chili sauce
1 14-ounce jar of duck sauce
2 tablespoons soy sauce
2 tablespoons dry mustard

Rub the skinned drumsticks thoroughly and place in a single layer in a shallow baking dish. Mix the remaining ingredients in a sauce pan and bring to a boil. Pour the sauce over the chicken and bake at 375 degrees for one hour.

FRAYDA FAIGEL AND HARRIS FAIGEL

Fish Cocktail

1 pound cooked white flesh fish – cod, haddock or halibut
½ cup ketchup
¼ teaspoon salt
¼ cup chili sauce
1 tablespoon horseradish
1 teaspoon Worcestershire sauce
½ teaspoon Tabasco sauce
½ teaspoon kosher salt
Crackers, celery, red pepper or endive leaves

Cut the fish into ½ inch cubes. Combine the remaining ingredients to make a sauce and add the fish. Chill. Serve on crackers, celery, endive or sweet red pepper strips.

~~

Chicken Canapé

½ pound roasted chicken breast, finely chopped. Leftover meat from a roasted chicken works well.
¼ cup slivered almonds, toasted
½ cup dry sherry
½ teaspoon kosher salt
¼ teaspoon freshly ground black pepper

Using the leftover meat from a roast chicken, finely chop the meat in a mortar with the slivered almonds. Add sherry until the mixture forms a smooth paste. Add salt and pepper and chill. Serve on rye crisps or vegetables.

Chapter X - Soups

Vegetarian Kale And Bean Soup

Serves 6

1 tablespoon polyunsaturated oil
8 cloves garlic, minced
1 onion, diced
4 cups kale
4 cups low salt vegetable stock
2 15-ounce cans cannellini beans
1 2 x 3 inch piece parmigiano regiano rind
2 large white potatoes, peeled, cubed and boiled for 10 minutes
3 cups diced tomatoes, drained
1 teaspoon dried oregano
1 teaspoon dried basil
1 teaspoon dried thyme
1 teaspoon kosher salt
1 teaspoon freshly ground black pepper
1 cup Romano cheese, freshly grated

Heat the oil in a casserole, add the garlic and onion and
sauté until translucent. Add the kale and sauté until it is
wilted. Add 2 cups of stock, 1 can of beans and the
parmigiano rind. Add the potatoes, tomatoes, oregano, basil,
thyme, salt and pepper and simmer for 5 minutes.

Place the remaining beans and stock in a blender and
puree until smooth. Stir into the soup to thicken it and
simmer for 15 minutes. Remove the cheese rind before
serving. Garnish each bowl with the grated cheese.

Tuscan Bread Soup

Serves 6

2 teaspoons extra virgin oil
1 white onion, grated
1 carrot, grated
1 rib celery, chopped
1 clove garlic, minced
1 large Idaho potato, peeled and diced
4 cups shredded green cabbage
1 bunch spinach, chopped
2 cups canned diced tomatoes with juice
1½ quarts low salt chicken stock
2 cups canned cannelloni beans
2 teaspoons kosher salt
1 teaspoon freshly ground black pepper
½ pound stale Italian bread in ½ inch slices
¼ cup grated Parmesan cheese

Heat the oil in a casserole over medium heat and sauté the onion, carrot and celery until soft. Add the potato, cabbage and spinach and cook for another 5 minutes.

Stir in the tomatoes and stock and bring to a boil. Reduce the heat to low and simmer for 30 minutes. Add the beans, salt and pepper and simmer for 15 minutes more.

Add the bread in layers, cover the pot and simmer for one hour. Sprinkle with cheese when serving.

~~

Pea Soup

Serves 6

1 16-ounce package dried split peas, washed and drained
3 quarts water
6 beef bouillon cubes
¾ cup finely chopped onions
½ cup finely chopped carrots
1 teaspoon kosher salt
¼ teaspoon freshly ground black pepper

Bring the water to a boil in a large kettle. Stir in the bouillon cubes, split peas, onion, carrots, salt and pepper. Return to a boil, then reduce the heat, cover and simmer for 2 hours.

For a thicker soup, simmer for 30 to 60 minutes more.

Beet Borscht

Serves 4

12 medium beets
2 quarts water
Juice of one lemon
2 tablespoons sugar
1 teaspoon kosher salt
2 eggs, whites only
Nonfat plain yogurt

Wash the beets and parboil to remove the skin easily. Reserve the liquid.

Grate the beets on a coarse grater and return to the reserved liquid. Add lemon juice, sugar and salt. Simmer for ½ hour.

Stir the egg whites until smooth. While stirring, slowly pour ½ cup of the borscht into the egg whites to avoid curdling. Pour the borscht and egg white mixture into the rest of the borscht.

Chill. Serve cold with a tablespoon of yogurt floating in the middle of the bowl.

~~

New England Fish Chowder

Serves 4

2 tablespoons polyunsaturated oil
½ cup chopped onions
½ pound halibut or other chowder fish, cubed
1 cup diced potatoes
3 cups bottled clam juice
¼ teaspoon white pepper
2 cups hot nonfat milk
1 tablespoon minced parsley
Crackers

Sauté the onions in the oil until soft and translucent. Add the fish and cook for 1 minute. Add the clam juice, potatoes and pepper and cook slowly over low heat for 20 minutes. Stir in the milk and parsley and simmer gently (do not let the chowder boil). Serve with crackers.

Turkey Soup

Serves 4

Carcass of one roasted turkey with the meat removed
1 parsnip, peeled and cut into 1 inch pieces
2 large carrots, peeled and cut into 1 inch pieces
4 celery ribs with the leaves, cut into 3 inch pieces
1 bay leaf
1 teaspoon dried thyme
1 teaspoon dried parsley
Water to cover

Place the turkey carcass, parsnip, carrots, celery in a large soup pot. Place the bay leaf, thyme and parsley in a tea ball and add to the soup pot. Add enough water to cover the ingredients. Bring to a boil, cover and reduce the heat. Simmer 3 hours. Discard the carcass. Strain the liquid, remove the tea ball and discard the cooked vegetables. Serve hot.

~~

Cioppino

Serves 6

¼ cup polyunsaturated oil
3 garlic cloves, chopped
1½ cups chopped onion
¾ cup chopped scallions
¾ cup chopped green pepper
1 jar whole clams, drained, liquid reserved
1 28-ounce can diced tomatoes
1 6-ounce can tomato paste
1¾ cup dry red wine
⅓ cup chopped parsley
½ teaspoon dry basil
½ teaspoon dry oregano
2 teaspoons kosher salt
¼ teaspoon freshly ground black pepper
¾ cup water
1½ pound halibut steak
½ pound medium shrimp, shelled and deveined
3 6½-ounce cans of king crabmeat, drained
Rice

Sauté the garlic, onion and green pepper in the oil in a 6 quart kettle until tender. Add the clam liquid, diced tomatoes, tomato paste, wine, parsley, basil, oregano, salt, pepper and water, mix well and bring to a boil. Reduce the heat and simmer uncovered for 10 minutes.

Remove the skin and bones from the halibut, cut into 1-inch chunks and add to the mixture.

Add the clams, shrimp and crab and simmer covered for 15 minutes and then uncovered for 15 minutes more.

Serve hot over rice.

~~

Vegetarian Garden Tomato Soup

Serves 4

3 pounds plum tomatoes, top ¼ inch cut off
1 medium onion, chopped
4 whole garlic cloves
2 cups low salt vegetable stock
2 tablespoons polyunsaturated margarine
2 tablespoons all-purpose flour
1 teaspoon kosher salt
¼ teaspoon freshly ground black pepper
1 teaspoon sugar
Fresh basil

In one quart of boiling water, scald the tomatoes in batches for 2 minutes each and then immerse in ice water. Squeeze the base of each tomato to remove the skin and halve each tomato.

In a large kettle over medium heat, combine the tomatoes, onion, garlic and vegetable stock and bring it to a boil. Reduce the heat to medium and boil gently for 20 minutes.

Remove the soup from the heat and cool for 15 minutes. In a blender, puree the soup until it is smooth.

In the empty kettle, melt the margarine. Stir in the flour to make a roux and continue cooking until the roux browns. Whisk one cup of the soup mixture into the roux until smooth and then stir in the remaining mixture. Stir in the salt, pepper and sugar. Garnish with fresh basil.

Gazpacho

Serves 6

¾ cup polyunsaturated oil
4 garlic cloves, crushed
½ medium onion, diced
1½ teaspoons kosher salt
½ cup vinegar
½ cup red wine
3 ripe beefsteak tomatoes
1 16-ounce can whole tomatoes
1 24-ounce can tomato juice
1 large ripe avocado
Chives, chopped
Green pepper
mushrooms

Make the soup in 2 batches.

In a bowl, combine the oil, garlic, onion, salt, vinegar and wine. Place half in a blender and fill to ⅔ with 1 tomato, ½ the avocado and half the canned tomato and tomato juice. Blend at full speed for 2 minutes and place in a large container. Repeat with the rest of the ingredients and mix the batches together.

Serve cold garnished with chives, chopped tomatoes, green peppers and mushrooms.

~~

Spinach Borscht

Serves 4

1 pound fresh or frozen spinach
2 quarts water
Juice of 2 lemons
3 tablespoons sugar
1 teaspoon kosher salt
¼ cup liquid egg substitute
1 cucumber, peeled and diced
1 cup plain yogurt

Add the spinach to the water, bring to a boil and simmer for 10 minutes. Add the lemon juice, sugar and salt. Pour 1 cup of soup into the egg substitute and return the combination to the soup.

Chill. Serve cold with a tablespoon of diced cucumber and plain yogurt in each bowl.

~~

Chicken Soup

Serves 4

1 5-pound chicken, washed, giblets removed
1 parsnip, cut in half
1 large carrot, cut in half
2 celery ribs, cut in half
Water to cover

Place all ingredients in a large soup pot. Add water to cover, bring to a boil, reduce the heat, cover and simmer for 2½ hours. Remove the chicken from the pot and reserve. Using a slotted spoon, remove the vegetables from the pot. Serve hot.

Remove all the meat from the chicken carcass. It can be served in the soup or made into chicken salad, chicken tacos or chicken pot pie

~~

French Onion Soup

Serves 6

1½ pounds white onions, sliced
½ cup extra virgin olive oil
2½ quarts low salt beef stock
½ teaspoon kosher salt
¼ teaspoon freshly ground black pepper

Sauté the onions in the olive oil over low heat until translucent and golden. Slowly blend in the beef stock, salt and pepper. Bring to a boil, cover, reduce the heat and simmer for 15 minutes.

Tomato Bisque

Serves 6

2 16-ounce cans whole tomatoes
2 beef bouillon cubes
1 tablespoon sugar
1 teaspoon kosher salt
1 teaspoon onion powder
¼ teaspoon dried basil
¼ teaspoon ground white pepper
1 bay leaf
½ cup polyunsaturated margarine
½ cup unsifted white flour
4 cups nonfat milk

Drain the tomatoes and reserve the liquid. Cut 1 cup of tomatoes into large pieces and reserve.

Combine the remaining tomatoes, liquid, bouillon cubes, sugar, salt, onion powder, basil, pepper and bay leaf in a kettle and simmer for 30 minutes.

Remove the bay leaf and force the mixture through a sieve.

Melt the margarine over low heat and blend in the flour. Gradually add the milk and cook over medium heat. Stir constantly until the mixture comes to a boil and remove from the heat. Gradually blend in the tomato and herb mixture. Add the tomato pieces and return to the heat.

Stir until hot.

~~

Minestrone

Serves 8

1 cup dry navy beans
1 quart water
1 cup onions, finely chopped
3 tablespoons polyunsaturated oil
3 quarts low salt beef stock
1 cup diced potatoes
1 cup shredded cabbage
1 tablespoon kosher salt
½ teaspoon freshly ground black pepper
1 teaspoon dry basil
8 ounces frozen green beans
2 teaspoons dry oregano

[82]

2 tablespoons chopped fresh parsley
½ cup diced green peppers
1 cup diced carrots
½ cup tomato paste
4 ounces macaroni

Boil the navy beans in 1 quart of water for 1½ hours.

Sauté the onions in oil in a heavy kettle until soft and translucent. Add the cooked beans and all the ingredients except for the macaroni. Bring to a boil, reduce the heat and simmer for 2½ hours or until the beans are soft. Add the macaroni and cook for 8 to 10 minutes until the macaroni is *al dente*. Serve hot.

~~

Beef And Barley Soup

Serves 4

2 tablespoons polyunsaturated oil
1 pound boneless chuck, trimmed of all visible fat, cut into ½ inch cubes
1 pound carrots, diced
1 cup celery, diced
½ cup onion, diced
2 cloves garlic, chopped
1 8-ounce package sliced mushrooms
¼ teaspoon marjoram
6 cups low salt beef stock
1 bay leaf
1 cup uncooked pearl barley
1 teaspoon kosher salt
½ teaspoon freshly ground black pepper

Heat the oil in a large Dutch oven over medium heat, add the meat and brown on all sides. Remove the meat from the pot, add the carrots, celery, onion, garlic, marjoram and mushrooms and cook, stirring occasionally until the liquid is reduced by three fourths. Add the beef, stock and bay leaf, cover and simmer for 90 minutes. Stir in the barley and simmer covered for 30 minutes. Remove the bay leaf and add the salt and pepper.

Catalonian Fish Soup

Serves 6

3 tablespoons polyunsaturated oil
3 large garlic cloves, diced
1 large tomato, peeled and chopped
1 pound yellow potatoes, thinly sliced
½ cup white wine
1½ cups low salt chicken stock
¾ teaspoon sugar
1 teaspoon kosher salt
¾ pound skinless halibut or monkfish
¼ pound large shrimp, peeled
10 marcona almonds, chopped and toasted
1 tablespoon flat leaf parsley, chopped

Heat the oil in a large casserole. Add the garlic and tomatoes and cook over medium heat for 20 minutes until the tomatoes disintegrate and thicken. Add the potatoes, wine, stock, sugar and salt and simmer covered for 20 minutes. Add the almonds, fish and shrimp and cook for 3 to 5 minutes until the shrimp turn pink and the fish is entirely white. Garnish with parsley.

~~

Italian Cabbage Soup

Serves 6

1 15-ounce can cannellini beans, drained
3 quarts low salt chicken stock
6 cloves garlic, minced
2 bay leaves
1 teaspoon dried sage
1 teaspoon dried basil
1 teaspoon kosher salt
½ cup extra virgin olive oil
2 medium onions, diced
2 large carrots, peeled and diced
2 large celery stalks, diced
2 medium white potatoes, peeled and diced
1½ cups green cabbage, chopped
2 cups kale, trimmed and chopped
1 can diced tomatoes, drained
12 slices Italian bread, toasted
2 cups grated Parmesan cheese
¼ cup Israeli couscous

Place the beans, stock, garlic, bay leaves, sage, basil and salt in a large casserole and bring to a boil. Reduce the heat to low and simmer for 15 minutes. Cool, remove 1 cup of beans and discard the bay leaves. Puree the remaining soup in a food processor until smooth and set aside.

Heat the rest of the olive oil in a large pot, add the onions and sauté until the onions are translucent. Stir in the, carrots, celery, potatoes, cabbage, kale and tomatoes, cover and cook over low heat for 15 minutes. Stir in the pureed beans, couscous and bread and cook for 30 more minutes. Garnish each serving with grated cheese.

~~

Sweet Potato Soup

Serves 6

3 tablespoons polyunsaturated oil
1 pound sweet potatoes, peeled and cubed
1 cup sweet white onion, diced
2½ cups water
2 cups low salt chicken stock
¾ pound chopped carrots
¼ cup yogurt
1 teaspoon kosher salt
½ teaspoon freshly ground black pepper
¼ teaspoon ground cinnamon
⅓ cup low-fat sour cream

Add 1 tablespoon polyunsaturated oil to a Dutch oven over medium heat. Add the onion and cook for 3 to 4 minutes until translucent. Add the remaining oil and the sweet potatoes, water, chicken stock and carrots. Bring to a boil, cover and reduce the heat and simmer for 15 minutes or until the potatoes and carrots are soft. Allow the soup to cool. Using an immersion blender, puree the soup until smooth. Stir in the yogurt, salt pepper and cinnamon. Serve cool with a tablespoon of sour cream floating in the middle of the bowl.

FRAYDA FAIGEL AND HARRIS FAIGEL

Vegetable Soup

Serves 4

2 quarts low salt vegetable stock
2 teaspoons kosher salt
1 large sweet potato, diced
1 medium white potato, peeled and diced
3 carrots, peeled and diced
2 celery ribs, diced
1 turnip, peeled and diced
1 medium white onion, diced
8 ounces fresh or frozen green beans, cut into ½ inch pieces
1 28-ounce can whole tomatoes
½ teaspoon freshly ground black pepper
½ teaspoon garlic powder
2 teaspoons chopped fresh parsley

Place all ingredients in a large pot. Bring to a boil, cover and simmer for 1½ to 2 hours until the vegetables are tender.

~~

Beef And Cabbage Borscht

Serves 6

2 pounds lean boneless chuck beef, cut into ½ inch cubes
5 medium beets, peeled and sliced
2 medium carrots, diced
2 medium onions, diced
1 28-ounce can diced tomatoes
3 stalks celery, diced
1 green pepper, diced
1 head green cabbage, diced
2 6-ounce cans tomato paste
1 teaspoon sour salt
2 bay leaves
1 teaspoon kosher salt
2 tablespoons sugar

Cover the meat with water and boil for 10 minutes.

Add the beets, carrots, onions, tomatoes, celery, green pepper, sour salt, bay leaves, kosher salt and sugar. Boil for 10 minutes. Add the tomato paste and cabbage and simmer for 3 hours. Skim fat from the surface of the soup. Serve hot.

Roasted Tomato Soup

Serves 4

4 pounds plum tomatoes, halved
4 garlic cloves, peeled, halved and crushed
½ cup extra virgin olive oil
½ teaspoon kosher salt
¼ teaspoon freshly ground white pepper
1 teaspoon dried thyme
1 teaspoon dried basil
1 teaspoon dried oregano
2 teaspoons sugar
2 ounces fresh basil leaves
16 ounces low salt chicken stock
½ cup oyster crackers

Spread the plum tomatoes and garlic on a baking tray and sprinkle with olive oil, salt, pepper, thyme, oregano and basil. Bake at 300 degrees for one hour. Cool the tomatoes and puree in a food processor until smooth. Add the fresh basil and pulse the processor enough to chop the basil. Add the chicken stock.

Serve hot and garnish with the oyster crackers.

~~

Algerian Zucchini Soup

Serves 6

1 cup extra virgin olive oil
3 medium sweet onions, diced
2 baking potatoes, peeled and diced
2 large zucchini, diced
½ cup tomato paste
6 cups water
Juice of 3 Meyer lemons
2 bunches cilantro, coarsely chopped
1 teaspoon kosher salt

In a large soup pot, heat the oil over medium heat and sauté the onions until translucent. Add the potatoes, zucchini, tomato paste and water, cover and cook over low heat for 30 minutes. When the potatoes are knife-soft, turn off the heat, add the lemon juice, cilantro and salt and puree in a blender or with an immersion blender to a thick smooth consistency. Serve cold.

Chapter XI - Meats

Ground Beef

Stuffed Romaine

Serves 6

4 ounces frozen spinach, defrosted
2 teaspoons kosher salt
1 medium onion, diced
¾ pound extra lean ground beef
½ cup uncooked white rice
1 teaspoon spicy chili sauce
½ cup chopped fresh mint
½ cup chopped fresh flat leaf parsley
½ cup liquid egg substitute
1 tablespoon extra virgin olive oil
2 large heads of romaine lettuce
Sauce
¼ cup extra virgin olive oil
4 cloves garlic diced
1½ cups canned crushed tomatoes
6 cups water
½ teaspoon kosher salt
½ teaspoon freshly ground white pepper

In a bowl, combine the spinach, 1 teaspoon salt and onion. Rinse off the salt and squeeze dry.

In a mixing bowl, combine the meat, rice, chili sauce, mint, parsley, egg substitute, remaining salt and pepper and then stir in the spinach and onion mixture.

Cut off the bottom stems of the romaine and blanch in boiling water in a large pot for 20-30 seconds. Remove with tongs and plunge into ice water to stop the cooking.

Shave the stems from the middle of each leaf to make them easier to roll. Place a leaf with the rib side down, place 2 heaping tablespoons of the meat near the bottom of the leaf, loosely roll the bottom, tuck in the sides, and finish rolling the leaf. Secure each leaf with a toothpick and place the rolled leaf on a plate, seam side down.

Make the sauce by heating the oil over medium heat in the pot used to blanch the romaine, add the garlic, heat for 1 minute and then stir in the tomatoes, 3 cups of water, salt and pepper and simmer for 10 minutes. Add the stuffed romaine to the broth in two layers and add the remaining water. Bring the sauce to a boil, reduce the heat and simmer for 1 hour. Serve with broth spooned over the romaine.

~~

Baked Stuffed Eggplant

Serves 4

8 small eggplants cut in half lengthwise
2 cloves garlic, finely chopped
½ cup polyunsaturated oil
1 teaspoon kosher salt
½ teaspoon dry oregano
½ teaspoon dry basil
½ teaspoon dry rosemary
¾ cup plain breadcrumbs
½ cup liquid egg substitute
1 pound extra lean ground beef
Lemon wedges

Scoop the pulp from the eggplant and reserve the shells. Dice the pulp and reserve.

Sauté the garlic in the oil until translucent. Add the eggplant pulp and sauté until soft. Add the salt, oregano, basil and rosemary. Mix thoroughly. Remove from the heat and add the liquid egg substitute and breadcrumbs and mix.

Brown the ground beef under a broiler, drain off the fat and add to the eggplant mixture.

Stuff the eggplant shells with the eggplant and meat mixture. Bake at 400 degrees for one hour.

Serve with lemon wedges.

Chili

Serves 6

2 20-ounce cans kidney beans
¼ cup polyunsaturated margarine
1½ cups chopped onion
1 tablespoon minced garlic
1 pound extra lean ground round steak
1½ cups water
1½ teaspoons kosher salt
1½ to 3 teaspoons chili powder

Drain the beans and reserve 2 cups of the liquid (add sufficient water to make 2 cups if needed).

Heat the margarine in a large saucepan and brown the meat. Pour off the excess fat. Stir in the reserved bean liquid, water, salt and chili powder. Bring the mixture to a boil, cover and simmer, stirring occasionally, for 30 minutes. Uncover, add the beans and continue cooking, stirring occasionally, for 5 minutes.

Serve hot.

~~

Beef And Spanish Rice

Serves 4

¼ cup polyunsaturated oil
1 medium onion, diced
½ medium green pepper, diced
½ pound extra lean ground beef
1½ cups instant rice
2 8-ounce cans tomato sauce
1½ cups hot water
1 teaspoon kosher salt
1 teaspoon prepared yellow mustard
¼ teaspoon freshly ground black pepper

Stir the onion, green pepper, beef and rice in the oil in a skillet over medium heat until the meat is browned. Drain off the excess oil. Add the tomato sauce and the remaining ingredients. Mix well and bring to a boil. Reduce the heat and simmer uncovered for 5 minutes

Zucchini Lasagna

Serves 6

1 cup chopped onion
¼ pound extra lean ground beef
½ tablespoon polyunsaturated oil
1 15-ounce can tomato sauce
½ teaspoon kosher salt
½ teaspoon dry oregano
½ teaspoon dry basil
¼ teaspoon dried rosemary
¼ teaspoon freshly ground black pepper
1 medium zucchini sliced lengthwise into ¼ inch thick slices
1 8-ounce container of low fat cottage cheese
1 tablespoon polyunsaturated oil
2 tablespoons all-purpose flour
¼ pound low fat mozzarella cheese, shredded

Preheat the oven to 375 degrees.

Sauté the onion and ground beef in ½ tablespoon oil in a 10 inch skillet over medium heat until translucent. Spoon off all of the excess fat. Add the tomato sauce, kosher salt, oregano, basil, rosemary and pepper and bring to a boil. Reduce the heat and simmer for 15 minutes.

In a small bowl, combine the egg substitute and cottage cheese.

Grease the bottom of a 12 x 8 inch baking dish with polyunsaturated oil. Spread a thin layer of the meat and tomato sauce in the dish. Arrange half the zucchini slices in the dish. Top with half of the cottage cheese mixture.

Sprinkle with one tablespoon flour. Spread a thin layer of tomato sauce. Arrange the remaining zucchini slices on top of the cottage cheese. Sprinkle with one tablespoon of flour. Top with the remaining cottage cheese mixture. Spread the remaining tomato sauce. Sprinkle with the mozzarella cheese.

Bake at 375 degrees for 45 minutes until hot and bubbly and the zucchini is fork-tender. Let stand and cool for 10 minutes for easier cutting.

Sweet And Sour Meatballs

Serves 8

2 pounds extra lean ground turkey breast
¼ cup liquid egg substitute
1 large onion, grated
¼ teaspoon kosher salt
¼ teaspoon garlic powder
2 tablespoons lemon juice
1 10-ounce jar grape jelly
1 12-ounce jar chili sauce

Mix the meat, egg substitute, onion, kosher salt and garlic powder. Use a small fruit-baller and form small meat balls. Cook the meatballs in a mixture of lemon juice, grape jelly and chili sauce for 30 minutes. Serve over rice.

~~

Madrileno Cheese-Stuffed Eggplant

Serves 4

2 eggplants, halved lengthwise
3 tablespoons extra virgin olive oil
4 shallots, diced
2 cloves garlic, minced
2 tablespoons fresh flat leaf parsley, minced
1 cup unseasoned bread crumbs
2 tablespoons chopped fresh chives
½ teaspoon dried basil
½ teaspoon dried oregano
¼ teaspoon dried cilantro
1 teaspoon kosher salt
½ teaspoon freshly ground black pepper
1 cup ricotta cheese
½ cup liquid egg substitute
¼ cup walnut halves, toasted
2 tablespoons chopped capers
½ cup sliced black olives

Scoop out the cores of the eggplants leaving a ½ inch thick shell. Chop and reserve the pulp. Cook the shells in salted boiling water for 3 minutes.

Sauté the shallots and garlic in 2 tablespoons of olive oil over medium heat in a large skillet for 5 minutes. Add the remaining olive oil and the chopped eggplant pulp and parsley. Sauté for 10 minutes. Remove from the stove and stir in the bread crumbs, chives, basil, oregano, cilantro, salt and pepper. Add the cheese, egg substitute and walnuts.

Stuff the eggplant shells with the mixture, cover with aluminum foil and bake at 350 degrees for 20 minutes. Uncover and bake for 10 minutes more until the stuffing is crisp and golden brown.

~~

Stuffed Cabbage

Serves 6

1 large green cabbage
1½ pounds extra lean ground chuck
1 medium onion, chopped
1 cup cooked white rice
1 teaspoon kosher salt
¼ teaspoon freshly ground black pepper
1 28-ounce can whole tomatoes
2 6-ounce cans tomato paste
¾ cup water
¼ cup seedless raisins
3 tablespoons brown sugar
3 tablespoons white vinegar
5 bay leaves

Remove the core of the cabbage and boil in water for 10 minutes until tender. Remove the cabbage and immerse in ice water. When chilled, separate the leaves.

Mix the ground meat, rice, onion, salt, pepper and 4 teaspoons of tomato paste together. Place 1½ tablespoons of the mixture in a cabbage leaf. Tuck the sides of the leaf in, tuck one end and then roll.

Place each roll sealed side down in a large baking dish. Continue until all the leaves are filled.

Mix the remainder of the tomato paste, tomatoes, water, raisins, brown sugar and vinegar and pour over the cabbage rolls.

Add the bay leaves. Simmer covered for 3 hours.
Serve hot or cold.

FRAYDA FAIGEL AND HARRIS FAIGEL

Lima Bake

Serves 6

1 pound dry lima beans
2 quarts water
2 teaspoons kosher salt
¾ pound extra lean ground beef
1 medium onion, finely chopped
3 tablespoons polyunsaturated oil
2 8-ounce cans tomato sauce
¼ teaspoon seasoned salt

Wash the beans and soak in 2 quarts of water overnight.

Simmer the beans in the same water for 1½ hours the next morning. Add 2 teaspoons kosher salt after the first ½ hour of cooking. Drain the beans and reserve ½ cup of the liquid. Place the beans in a casserole

In a skillet, brown the meat in the oil. Drain the excess fat and oil. Add the tomato sauce and the remaining ingredients, mix and pour over the beans.

Bake at 350 degrees for 1 hour. Serve hot.

~~

Stuffed Peppers

Serves 6

6 medium green peppers
2 teaspoon kosher salt
3 quarts water
¾ cup sliced onions plus ½ cup chopped onion
2 tablespoons polyunsaturated margarine
2 8-ounce cans tomato sauce
1 8-ounce can diced tomatoes
¼ cup lemon juice
3 tablespoons honey
1½ teaspoons kosher salt
1 pound extra lean ground beef
1 cup cooked rice
¼ teaspoon freshly ground black pepper
1½ teaspoons Worcestershire sauce

Remove the tops, seeds and veins in the peppers. Cook the peppers in salted boiling water for 3 minutes, plunge into ice water, drain and reserve.

Sauté the sliced onions in 1 tablespoon of margarine until translucent. Add 1 can of tomato sauce, diced tomatoes, lemon juice, honey and ¼ teaspoon kosher salt to a 2 quart casserole.

Melt the remaining margarine in a sauté pan and brown the ground meat and chopped onion over medium heat. Drain off the excess fat. Stir in the remaining tomato sauce, rice, remaining kosher salt, pepper and Worcestershire sauce.

Spoon the meat mixture into the green peppers. Stand the peppers in the casserole, cut side up. Bake at 400 degrees for 30 minutes. Spoon the sauce in the casserole over the peppers before serving.

~~
Meat Loaf

Serves 6

2 pounds extra lean ground beef
1½ cups flavored bread crumbs
1 small onion, finely chopped
1½ teaspoons dry basil
¼ cup fresh parsley, finely chopped
2 garlic cloves, minced
½ cup liquid egg substitute
¼ cup water
⅓ cup Ketchup
1 tablespoon Worcestershire sauce
1 teaspoon kosher salt
½ teaspoon freshly ground black pepper

Combine all the ingredients in a large bowl and mix thoroughly. Shape into a loaf and place in a 3 x 5 x 9 inch loaf pan.

Bake at 350 degrees for 1 hour.

Drain off the fat, cool slightly, place on serving dish and slice.

Special Hash

Serves 6

1 pound extra lean ground beef
2 large white onions, sliced
2 green peppers, seeded and finely chopped
2 tablespoons polyunsaturated oil
2 cups canned tomatoes
½ cup instant cooked rice
1 teaspoon chili sauce
1 teaspoon onion powder
2 teaspoons kosher salt
¼ teaspoon freshly ground black pepper

Sauté the meat, onion and green peppers in the oil until the vegetables are soft and the meat loses its pinkness. Drain off the excess fat. Add the remaining ingredients, mix and pour into a casserole.

Bake at 350 degrees for 45 minutes.

~~

Lima Brisket

Serves 6

2 16-ounce cans lima beans
1 4-pound center-cut brisket, trimmed of visible fat
1 package onion soup mix
1 medium onion, chopped
2 cloves garlic, diced
3 tablespoons ketchup
2 tablespoons molasses
1 tablespoon lemon juice
1 teaspoon kosher salt
½ teaspoon freshly ground black pepper
4 ginger snaps

Place all the ingredients except for the ginger snaps in a Dutch oven, cover and bake at 350 degrees for 3 hours or until the meat is fork tender. Add water during cooking to ensure that the meat remains covered. Soften the ginger snaps in 1 teaspoon of water, add to the Dutch oven and return to the oven for 10 more minutes.

Beef

Beef Bourguignon

Serves 8

1 head of garlic
2 tablespoons dry red wine
4 tablespoons bacon-flavored bits
3½ pounds boneless flank steak cut into 1½ inch thick pieces
¼ cup polyunsaturated oil
1 large onion, chopped
1 large carrot, chopped
1 celery rib, diced
3 tablespoons flour
4 tablespoons tomato paste
1 teaspoon thyme
1 teaspoon sage
1 teaspoon oregano
1 teaspoon rosemary
3 bay leaves
2 cups dry red wine
3 cups low salt beef stock
12 ounces canned pearl onions
12 ounces shiitake mushrooms, stemmed and quartered

Cut the top ½ inch from the garlic head. Place the garlic in a piece of foil, pour 2 tablespoons of wine over the garlic, wrap in foil and roast for 45 minutes. Cool the garlic and press to remove the garlic from the skin.

Working in batches, brown the meat in the oil over medium high heat until dark and crispy and then set aside. Drain off any fat from the pan. Reduce the heat to medium low and add the onion, carrot and celery and sauté until softened. Add the tomato paste, thyme, sage, oregano and rosemary and stir. Add the bay leaves and 2 cups of dry red wine and simmer for 15 minutes. Add the beef stock and the meat, cover and simmer for 1½ hours. Add the onions and mushrooms, cover and simmer for 15 minutes.

Roast Beef Tenderloin

Serves 8

6 pound choice beef tenderloin
¼ cup polyunsaturated oil
2 tablespoons kosher salt
2 tablespoons freshly ground black pepper
¼ teaspoon dry thyme
¼ teaspoon tarragon

Preheat the oven to 450 degrees.

Carefully remove excess fat from the beef. Rub the beef with the oil. Mix the salt, pepper, tarragon and thyme and rub it over the entire surface of the beef.

Place the beef on a rack in a roasting pan and roast the meat for 15 minutes.

Reduce the oven to 375 degrees and continue roasting until an instant thermometer reads 135 for rare. Remove the roast from the oven, cover with aluminum foil and let rest for 15 minutes before carving.

~~

Braised Beef Shanks

Serves 4

4 beef shanks, 2 inches thick
¼ cup polyunsaturated oil
2 pounds marrow bones
2 tablespoons flour
1 carrot, peeled and diced
1 stalk celery, diced
1 small onion, diced
5 cloves garlic, diced
4 tablespoons tomato paste
1 bottle dry red wine
16 ounces low salt beef stock
1 bay leaf
1 teaspoon kosher salt
½ teaspoon freshly ground black pepper

Place the flour and beef shanks in a large plastic freezer bag and shake well to coat the meat.

In a large Dutch oven, heat the oil until hot and then sear the meat and marrow bones until a brown crust forms. Remove to a platter. Pour off the remaining fat.

Over medium heat, add the carrot, celery, onion and garlic to the Dutch oven and sauté until softened. Add the tomato paste and cook for 3 minutes. Return the meat and marrow bones to the Dutch oven, add the bay leaf, salt, pepper, wine and stock, bring to a boil, cover and place the Dutch oven in a 300 degree oven. Cook for 3 hours until the meat is very tender. Remove the meat and bay leaf from the pot, puree the vegetables, bring the sauce to a boil and reduce by ⅓. Spoon the sauce over the meat and bones when served.

~~

Beef Stroganoff

Serves 8

4 pounds lean flank steak, cut into thin strips
2 teaspoons kosher salt
¼ teaspoon freshly ground black pepper
1 cup onion, finely chopped
4 cups water
4 beef bouillon cubes
1 pound mushrooms, sliced
2 tablespoons corn starch
2 cups low fat yogurt
6 tablespoons tomato paste
2 tablespoons Worcestershire sauce
Noodles

Dredge the meat in a mixture of salt and pepper and brown on a rack under a broiler. Place the meat in a deep baking dish. Add the onion, water, bouillon cubes and mushrooms. Cover and simmer for 25 minutes. Add cornstarch and stir until thickened.

Blend the remaining ingredients, add to the meat and stir. Serve over noodles.

Beef Teriyaki

Serves 6

1½ pounds lean flank steak, fat trimmed, and cut into thin strips
¼ cup soy sauce
¼ cup sherry
½ lemon, thinly sliced
1 clove garlic, crushed
3 tablespoons sugar
½ apple, grated
1 tablespoon polyunsaturated oil

Combine soy sauce, sherry, lemon, garlic and sugar with the grated apple. Pour over the meat, refrigerate and marinate for 3 hours or longer. Stir fry in the oil in a skillet or wok over moderate heat for 5-7 minutes.

~~

Beef With Pea Pods And Oyster Sauce

Serves 8

2 lean flank steaks (1½ pounds each)
1 cup polyunsaturated oil
1 tablespoon sherry
¼ cup soy sauce
2 tablespoons cornstarch
⅛ teaspoon fresh ground ginger
½ teaspoon sugar
2 scallions, chopped
½ pound fresh peapods
½ pound fresh mushrooms, sliced
2 tablespoons bottled oyster sauce

Very carefully trim all visible fat from the steaks and cut into 1½ inch thick slices. Toss in a bowl with 1 tablespoon of the oil, soy sauce, sherry, cornstarch, ginger, sugar and scallions. Marinate for one hour.

Trim the ends from the peapods. Slice the mushrooms.

In a skillet or wok, heat 9 tablespoons of oil until steaming. Add the flank steak mixture and stir fry for 4-5 minutes. Mix in the oyster sauce and remove to a heated platter.

Heat the remaining oil in the frying pan or wok, add the pea pods and mushrooms and stir fry to 2-3 minutes. Mix in the meat mixture and vegetables and serve.

~~

Goulash

Serves 8

4 pounds lean round steak, cut into 2 inch cubes
½ teaspoon kosher salt
¼ teaspoon freshly ground black pepper
½ teaspoon paprika
4 garlic cloves, minced
2 6-ounce cans tomato paste
1 cup water
8 cloves allspice
12 large potatoes, peeled and quartered

Brown the meat on a rack under the broiler and place in a large casserole. Season the meat with the salt, pepper and paprika. Stir and add the garlic, tomato paste, water and allspice. Cover and simmer for 2 hours. Add the potatoes and simmer for 45 minutes more.

~~

London Broil

Serves 8

1 4-pound London broil (chuck) cut thick
1 teaspoon garlic powder
1 14-ounce bottle chili sauce
2 large onions, sliced
2 medium tomatoes, sliced

Carefully trim all visible fat from the meat and place in a casserole. Sprinkle both sides with garlic powder. Pour the chili sauce over the London broil. Place the onions and tomato over the top, covering completely.

Bake at 450 degrees for one to 1½ hours, about 20 minutes per pound for rare meat. Slice at an angle across the grain.

Stuffed Flank Steak

Serves 4

2 tablespoons polyunsaturated oil
2 tablespoons finely chopped onion
1 cup coarsely chopped cooked green beans
1 can whole kernel corn, drained
3 tablespoons chopped pimiento
¼ teaspoon celery salt
⅛ teaspoon freshly ground black pepper
2 tablespoons bread crumbs
1 pound flank steak, ½ to ¾ inch thick.
1 12-ounce can tomato juice
1 beef bouillon cube
¼ cup dry red wine

In the oil, sauté the onion until it is translucent and tender. Add the beans, corn, pimiento, celery salt and pepper and simmer while stirring for 2 minutes. Drain the excess oil from the pan. Remove from the heat and add the bread crumbs.

Lay the steak in a baking dish. Spread the stuffing over the top. Bake at 350 degrees for 30 minutes.

Combine the tomato juice, bouillon cube and wine and pour over the steak. Bake for 15 minutes more.

~~

Braised Beef In Red Wine Sauce

Serves 8

2 pounds boneless chuck
1 cup orange juice
3 cups dry red wine
2 garlic cloves, peeled and thinly sliced
3 stalks celery cut into ½ inch pieces
2 carrots, peeled and cut into ½ inch pieces
2 white onions, peeled and diced
1½ cups low salt beef stock
⅓ cup extra virgin olive oil
½ teaspoon kosher salt
1 teaspoon freshly ground black pepper
2 tablespoons flour

Combine the orange juice, red wine, celery, carrots and onion in a large sealable plastic freezer bag. Add the meat and marinate in the refrigerator overnight.

Preheat the oven to 325 degrees. When ready to cook, remove the meat from the marinade and dust with flour on all sides. In a Dutch oven, warm the olive oil and when the oil is hot, sear the meat until a deep brown. Add the beef stock, salt, pepper and the marinade, cover the pot and place in the oven. Turn and baste the beef every 30 minutes for 3-4 hours until fork tender.

~~

Steak With Farro

Serves 4

2 cups farro
½ teaspoon kosher salt
¼ teaspoon freshly ground black pepper
⅓ cup chili sauce
12 stalks of asparagus, trimmed and cut into thirds
2 medium carrots, thinly sliced into coins
6 radishes, thinly sliced
¼ red onion, thinly sliced
8 thin slices of grilled flank steak, cut into thin slices

In a large sauce pan over high heat, combine the farro, salt and pepper. Add enough water to cover the farro by 2-3 inches, bring to a boil, reduce the heat and simmer for 25 to 30 minutes until the farro is tender and chewy. Drain the excess water and transfer to a serving bowl.

Heat 1 cup of water in a large skillet, bring to a simmer, add the asparagus and cook for 2 minutes until the asparagus is tender but still bright green. Plunge the asparagus into ice water just long enough to stop the cooking and then transfer to a plate.

Add the chili sauce, asparagus, carrots, radishes and onion to the cooked farro. Serve topped with slices of steak.

Braised Beef Short Ribs

Serves 8

4 pounds beef short ribs
2 teaspoons kosher salt
1 teaspoon freshly ground black pepper
12 shallots cut in half
1 carrot, shredded
1 celery rib, diced
4 cups dry red wine
3 tablespoons Dijon mustard
2 garlic cloves, minced
8 plum tomatoes, halved

Pat the beef ribs dry, cut into individual ribs and sprinkle with the salt and pepper. Brown the ribs in a skillet over medium high heat until dark and crusty. Remove the ribs from the skillet, drain off any fat and brown the shallots, carrot and celery. Stir in the wine and mustard, add the ribs and simmer covered for 2 hours. Add the garlic and tomatoes and simmer covered for 30 minutes. Place the ribs on a platter and spoon the sauce over the meat.

~~

Beef Stew

Serves 8

2 pounds lean boneless chuck cut into 1-inch cubes
2 cups beef stock
½ cup ketchup
1 tablespoon polyunsaturated oil
1 clove garlic, minced
1 bay leaf
1 teaspoon kosher salt
½ teaspoon freshly ground black pepper
3 medium potatoes, peeled and cut into 1-inch pieces
1½ cups carrot, cut in 1-inch pieces
1 cup celery cut in 1-inch pieces
1 cup white cannelloni beans

Carefully remove all visible fat from the meat and brown under the broiler. In a large saucepan, sauté the garlic in the oil until translucent. Add the meat, beef stock, ketchup, bay leaf, salt and pepper. Add the potatoes, carrot, celery and beans. Simmer for 2½ hours or until the meat is tender.

Heat 1 cup of water in a large skillet, bring to a simmer, add the asparagus and cook for 2 minutes until the asparagus is tender but still bright green. Plunge the asparagus into ice water just long enough to stop the cooking and then transfer to a plate.

Add the chili sauce, asparagus, carrots, radishes and onion to the cooked farro. Serve topped with slices of steak.

~~

Grilled Hanger Steak

Serves 6

½ teaspoon dry mustard
2 tablespoons low salt soy sauce
3 cloves garlic, minced
1 teaspoon dried thyme
2 teaspoons dried rosemary
Juice and zest of 1 lemon
2 teaspoons kosher salt
2 teaspoons freshly ground red peppercorns
½ cup dark beer
2 hanger steaks, trimmed, membrane removed

In a small bowl, whisk the mustard, soy sauce, garlic, thyme, rosemary, lemon juice and zest, salt and pepper until combined. Whisk in the beer.

Cut the hanger steaks in half lengthwise and place in a 1 gallon resealable plastic bag with the marinade. Seal the bag and marinate in the refrigerator overnight.

Remove the steaks from the bag and reserve the marinade. Grill the steaks over high heat for 4 minutes on each side, brushing regularly with the remaining marinade. Remove the steaks from the grill to a platter and cover with a tent of foil for 5 minutes. Slice across the grain when serving.

Sweet And Sour Brisket

Serves 8

6 pounds lean center cut brisket
2 onions, sliced
1 clove garlic, minced
¾ cup brown sugar
½ cup white vinegar
1 cup ketchup
1 cup water
1 tablespoon kosher salt
Freshly ground black pepper

Brown the brisket on all sides on a rack under the broiler and place in a heavy skillet. Add the onions, garlic and sauté until soft. Add the remaining ingredients. Simmer covered for 2½ to 3 hours or until tender.

~~

Plum And Apricot Tzimmes

Serves 8

2½ pounds lean beef chuck
¾ cup tomato juice
1 teaspoon kosher salt
½ teaspoon freshly ground black pepper
1 tablespoon brown sugar
6 white potatoes, quartered
3 large sweet potatoes, sliced
3 cups dried plums
1 cup dried apricots

Trim all visible fat from the beef, brown on a rack under a broiler and place in a large casserole. Add tomato juice to cover and simmer for one hour. Add the remaining ingredients and roast at 350 degrees for 2 hours until meat is tender and vegetables are drying out.

Pork

Italian Braised Pork Ribs

Serves 8

5 pounds lean country style pork spareribs
3 tablespoons polyunsaturated oil
1 large onion, diced
4 tablespoons flat leaf parsley, minced
2 bay leaves
1 garlic clove, diced
¼ teaspoon ground cloves
¼ teaspoon ground cinnamon
¼ teaspoon ground allspice
¼ teaspoon freshly ground black pepper
2 large cans diced tomatoes with juice
½ cup black olives, pitted
2 teaspoons dried basil
1 teaspoon kosher salt
1 teaspoon freshly ground black pepper

Trim all visible fat from the ribs and cut the ribs apart. Heat the oil in a sauté pan and brown the ribs slowly until dark and crusty and then remove from the pan.

Pour off all the fat and stir in the onion and parsley until the onion is translucent. Add the garlic, bay leaves, cloves, cinnamon, allspice and black pepper. Return the meat to the pan and stir until fully coated. Add the wine and deglaze the pan. Add the diced tomatoes. Stir in the olives, cover and simmer over low heat for one hour. Add the basil, salt and pepper, cover and cook for 45 minutes. Skim any remaining fat from the sauce before serving.

Caraway Pork

Serves 8

4 pounds lean boneless pork loin
2 teaspoons kosher salt
3 teaspoons caraway seeds
¼ teaspoon freshly ground black pepper
1 large garlic clove, crushed
½ cup water
2 large onions, cut in thick slices

Trim the pork of all visible fat and brown slowly and thoroughly on all sides in a large Dutch oven. Skim off the fat. Rub with salt, caraway seeds and pepper. Add the garlic and water, cover and simmer 2½ hours. Place the onion slices around the meat and simmer for 30 minutes. Serve each slice of meat with a slice of onion.

~~

Oven Roasted Pork Barbecue

Serves 8

1 5-pound lean boneless pork loin
1 medium onion, chopped
⅓ cup chopped celery
1 clove garlic, minced
2 tablespoons brown sugar
2 teaspoons Dijon mustard
1 small can tomato paste
½ cup low fat vegetable stock
2 tablespoons Worcestershire sauce
2 tablespoons white vinegar
¼ teaspoon Tabasco
2 16-ounce cans small whole white potatoes, drained

Carefully trim all visible fat from the pork loin. Roast the port uncovered on a rack in a shallow roasting pan for 2 hours. Combine the onion, celery, garlic, brown sugar, mustard, tomato paste, vegetable stock, vinegar, Worcestershire and Tabasco in a saucepan and simmer for 5 minutes. Drain the fat from the roasting pan, remove the pork from the rack and place it in the pan. Arrange the potatoes around the pork and spoon half the sauce over the pork and roast for 30 minutes. Pour the remaining sauce over the pork and roast for 30 minutes longer. Allow the pork to rest 10 minutes before slicing.

~~

Glazed Rolled Pork Roast

Serves 8

1 5-pound rolled lean pork loin
½ teaspoon kosher salt
¼ teaspoon freshly ground black pepper
¼ teaspoon allspice
2 medium oranges
3 whole cloves
¾ cup apricot jam
1 tablespoon flour
½ teaspoon dry mustard
3 teaspoons freshly grated orange peel

Carefully trim all visible fat from the surface of the pork. Place the pork open side down on a wire rack in a shallow roasting pan. Rub with salt, pepper and allspice and roast for 3 hours until a meat thermometer registers 185 degrees.

Cut the orange into ¼ inch thick slices and halve. Insert the cloves into the end peel and refrigerate.

Mix the apricot jam, flour, mustard and orange peel and set aside.

When the pork roast is done, remove from the oven and remove the butcher string. Make 12 slashes across the roast and spread each with apricot jam mixture. Insert one slice of orange into each slash. Spread the remaining apricot mixture over the oranges.

Roast at 400 degrees for 12 minutes until glazed.

Rosemary Pork Chops

Serves 4

4 pork chops, bone in, trimmed of visible fat
4 cloves garlic, sliced
½ teaspoon kosher salt
½ teaspoon freshly ground black pepper
1 tablespoon polyunsaturated oil
1 teaspoon dried rosemary
1 pound sliced mushrooms
⅓ cup dry white wine
Lemon slices

Make several slices in each pork chop and insert a slice of garlic into each. Rub the pork chops with salt and pepper. In a large skillet, cook the chops in the oil for 2 minutes over high heat until browned on both sides. Add the rosemary and cook for 5 to 6 minutes more until the chops are tender. Remove the chops from the pan and add the mushrooms. Sauté for 1 minute, add the wine and cook over medium heat for 5 minutes. Add the chops to the skillet and turn them to coat with the sauce. Garnish with lemon slices.

Lamb

Spiced Lamb Riblets

Serves 6

2 pounds of small lamb riblets
2 garlic cloves, minced
¼ teaspoon ground ginger
½ cup chili paste
¼ cup sugar
1 tablespoon low salt soy sauce
2 tablespoons sesame oil
½ teaspoon freshly ground black pepper

Combine the garlic, ginger, chili paste, sugar, soy sauce, sesame oil and pepper in a bowl. Cut the riblets into separate pieces, add to the bowl, mix to cover the meat entirely, cover with plastic wrap and refrigerate for 3 hours.

Grill the riblets over high heat for 3 minutes on each side.

~~

Braised Lamb With Lemon

Serves 8

2 pounds boneless lamb shoulder, trimmed of all fat and cut into 1½ inch cubes
2 garlic cloves, chopped
½ cup dry white wine
2 cups water
1 6-ounce can tomato paste
1½ teaspoons kosher salt
⅛ teaspoon freshly ground black pepper
1 teaspoon allspice
½ teaspoon cinnamon
1 teaspoon chopped parsley
2 medium onions, chopped
1 lemon, sliced
1 10-ounce package frozen artichoke hearts
Noodles

Heat a large skillet and coat with anti-stick spray. Brown the lamb pieces on all sides a few at a time and remove to a Dutch oven.

Drain any fat from the skillet and sauté the garlic until translucent. Pour in the wine and stir to loosen brown bits. Add the water and the tomato paste and bring to a boil.

Rub the lamb with the salt, pepper, allspice, cinnamon and parsley. Add the lamb, onions and the wine mixture to the Dutch oven. Add the lemon slices. Stir, cover and cook on medium heat for 2 hours. Add the artichoke hearts and cook for 15 minutes more.

Discard the lemon slices and remove the meat to a serving dish. Transfer the liquid to a sauce pan and skim the fat. Boil the liquid over medium heat until the liquid is reduced in volume by half and slightly thickened. Pour the sauce over the lamb and serve with noodles.

Butterflied Leg Of Lamb

Serves 8

8 garlic cloves, chopped
3 teaspoons dried thyme
2 teaspoons rosemary leaves, crumbled
1 cup oil-cured kalamata olives, pitted and chopped
2 tablespoons flat leaf parsley, chopped
1 tablespoon kosher salt
½ teaspoon freshly ground black pepper
3 tablespoons extra virgin olive oil
1 4-pound boneless leg of lamb, trimmed of all fat and butterflied
Juice of 1 lemon

In a small bowl, stir the garlic, thyme, rosemary, parsley and olives together. Cut slits into the lamb and rub the dry garlic mixture over the entire surface and into the pockets.

Grill on a barbeque for 10 minutes on each side or until an instant read thermometer reads 125 degrees. Remove the meat to a cutting board, squeeze the lemon juice over the meat, cover with foil and let stand for 15 minutes before serving.

~~

Shish Kabob 1

Serves 8

3 pounds leg of lamb, cubed
½ cup polyunsaturated oil
¾ cup lemon juice
2 tablespoons dry oregano
½ teaspoon freshly ground black pepper
6 medium tomatoes, quartered
3 medium onions, quartered
3 green bell peppers, quartered
1 pound mushroom caps

Mix the lemon juice, oregano, pepper and oil, rub over the lamb and refrigerate for 6 hours or more.

Skewer the lamb on its own skewers. Alternate the tomatoes, onions, green pepper and mushrooms on other skewers. Broil the vegetable skewers for 20 minutes, basting with the remaining marinade. Add the lamb skewers and broil for 10 minutes, basting with the remaining marinade.

~~

Braised Lamb Shanks

Serves 6

¼ cup polyunsaturated oil
6 lamb shanks
1 teaspoon kosher salt
1 teaspoon freshly ground black pepper
1 large celery stalk, diced
1 large onion, diced
1 large carrot, peeled and diced
6 cloves garlic, smashed
1 small tube anchovy paste
2 bay leaves
1 teaspoon dried thyme
1 teaspoon dried oregano
1 tablespoon tomato paste
1 bottle dry red wine
1 can low salt chicken stock

Heat the oil in a large cast iron pot over medium high heat. Rub the lamb shanks with the salt and pepper and sauté until brown on all sides. Remove the shanks from the pot to a plate and tent with aluminum foil. Add the celery, onion and carrot and sauté over medium heat until the onion is translucent. Add the garlic and sauté for 1 minute more until the garlic is translucent. Add the anchovy paste, bay leaves, thyme, oregano and tomato paste. Add the wine and chicken stock and boil until the liquid is reduced by ⅓. Return the lamb to the pot.

Cook the lamb uncovered in the oven at 325 degrees for two hours, basting occasionally. Transfer the lamb to a platter, skim the fat from the sauce and puree the vegetables and sauce in a food processor until thickened. Return the sauce and the lamb to the pot and bring to a boil before serving.

Shish Kabob 2

Serves 8

3 pounds leg of lamb, cubed
6 tablespoons lemon juice
4 tablespoons polyunsaturated oil
2 tablespoons minced onions
½ teaspoon cayenne
1 teaspoon ginger
½ teaspoon garlic powder
2 teaspoons curry powder
1 tablespoon kosher salt
2 onions, quartered
3 green peppers, quarters
3 tomatoes, quartered
8 mushroom caps

Marinate the meat for 6 hours or more in a mixture of lemon juice, oil, minced onion, cayenne, ginger, garlic powder, curry powder and salt.

Place the meat on skewers. On other skewers, alternate the green pepper, tomato and mushroom caps. Broil the skewered vegetables in a baking pan for 15 minutes. Then add the meat skewers and broil for 10 minutes more for rare, 12 for medium.

~~

Braised Lamb Shanks With White Beans

Serves 6

1 can cannellini beans drained and rinsed
2 tablespoons polyunsaturated oil
6 ½-pound lamb shanks
1 onion, diced
1 celery rib, diced
2 carrots, diced
8 garlic cloves, minced
2 cups red wine
1 cup low salt chicken stock
1½ cups canned diced tomatoes
4 tablespoons tomato paste
¼ teaspoon dried thyme
¼ teaspoon dried basil
1 bay leaf

1 teaspoon kosher salt
½ teaspoon freshly ground black pepper
1 tablespoon fresh lemon zest
3 tablespoons flat leaf parsley, chopped

Warm the olive oil in a Dutch oven over medium high heat and brown the lamb shanks on all sides for 12 minutes, 2 at a time and transfer to a plate. Add the onion, celery and carrots to the pan and sauté until tender. Add the garlic and cook, stirring for 2 minutes. Add the beans, wine, stock, tomatoes, tomato paste, thyme, basil and bay leaf. Add the lamb shanks, cover and simmer for 3½ hours. Season with the salt and pepper. Garnish with lemon zest and parsley.

FRAYDA FAIGEL AND HARRIS FAIGEL

Persian Lamb Stew

Serves 4

1 pound lean lamb trimmed of visible fat and cubed
1 tablespoon polyunsaturated oil
1 medium onion, finely chopped
½ teaspoon kosher salt
¼ teaspoon freshly ground black pepper
½ teaspoon ground cinnamon
½ teaspoon allspice
½ teaspoon dried thyme
2 tablespoons seedless raisins
4 ounces dried apricots, halved
1 small eggplant, cut in small pieces
1 small zucchini, cut in small pieces
Boiled rice
Water to cover

Brown the meat under the broiler on a rack in a large pan. Sauté the onion in a large casserole in the oil until golden and add the lamb. Season with the salt, pepper, cinnamon, thyme and allspice. Add the raisins, apricots, eggplant and zucchini. Cover with water and simmer gently, covered for 1½ hours. Serve over boiled rice.

Veal

Braised Veal Shoulder

Serves 8

4 pounds veal shoulder, boned, trimmed of fat, rolled and tied
1 teaspoon kosher salt
1 teaspoon freshly ground black pepper
⅓ cup polyunsaturated oil
2 large onions, diced
1 stalk celery, diced
1 carrot, peeled and diced
6 red peppercorns
1 bay leaf
¾ cup chopped parsley
2 garlic cloves
½ cup dry white wine
1 8-ounce can tomato sauce
½ cup low salt chicken stock
2 large onions, sliced
3 green peppers, seeded and diced
4 tablespoons polyunsaturated oil
1 small eggplant, peeled and cubed
1 16-ounce can of crushed tomatoes
2 teaspoons kosher salt
2 garlic cloves, minced

Season the veal with kosher salt and freshly ground
pepper and brown in oil in a Dutch oven. Remove the veal
from the pan and reserve.

Sauté the diced onion, celery and carrot in the Dutch oven
until they are soft. Drain the remaining oil. Add the bay leaf,
peppercorns, parsley, garlic cloves, wine, tomato sauce,
stock, veal and cook uncovered over medium heat. Baste with
more stock as needed for 2 hours.

Sauté the sliced onions and green pepper in 4 tablespoons
of oil in a skillet until they are golden. Add the zucchini,
eggplant, crushed tomatoes and salt. Cover and simmer for
15 minutes. Add the minced garlic and simmer for 2 minutes
more. Place the veal on a serving dish and surround with the
vegetables. Skim fat from the liquid in the Dutch oven and
serve as a sauce.

Barbecued Veal

Serves 8

3 pounds boneless veal breast
1 teaspoon kosher salt
1 teaspoon freshly ground black pepper
1 8-ounce can tomato sauce
½ cup chili sauce
½ cup water
1 medium onion, chopped
½ cup chopped celery
2 tablespoons brown sugar
2 tablespoons prepared mustard
1 tablespoon Worcestershire
2 cloves garlic, crushed
Brown rice

Trim all visible fat from the veal, cut into 2 inch pieces and brown on all sides on a rack under the broiler. Place in a casserole, season with the salt and pepper. Combine the remaining ingredients, pour over the meat, cover and bake at 350 degrees for 2½ hours.

Serve over brown rice.

~~

Rolled Veal

Serves 8

4 pounds veal shoulder, boned, rolled and tied
6 tablespoons all-purpose flour
1 tablespoon dry mustard powder
1 tablespoon brown sugar
2 teaspoons kosher salt
1 teaspoon poultry seasoning
¼ teaspoon freshly ground black pepper
2 tablespoons polyunsaturated oil
1 large onion, diced
¼ cup celery, chopped
2 tablespoons chopped flat leaf parsley
2 tablespoons cider vinegar
½ cup water
2 teaspoons prepared horseradish

Rub the veal with a mixture of 2 tablespoons flour, mustard, brown sugar, salt, poultry seasoning and pepper. Brown the meat slowly in the remaining oil in a Dutch oven. Add the onion, celery, parsley and vinegar. Cover and simmer 3 hours. Remove the meat to a carving board and cover with a tent of aluminum foil to keep warm.

Strain the stock into a 2-cup measure. Let the fat rise to the top and skim off all the fat. Add enough water to make 2 cups and return to the Dutch oven.

Smooth the remaining flour and water in a cup into a paste and stir into the stock mixture. Cook, stirring, until the gravy thickens and then boil for 1 minute. Stir in the horseradish to make a sauce.

~~

Breaded Veal Cutlets

Serves 4

1 pound thin veal cutlets
1 teaspoon kosher salt
1 teaspoon paprika
1 cup dry bread crumbs
1 tablespoon parsley
1 tablespoon dried basil
½ teaspoon garlic powder
½ cup liquid egg substitute
¼ cup polyunsaturated oil
1 lemon, sliced

Combine the salt and paprika and sprinkle evenly over the cutlets. Place the cutlets between two layers of wax paper and pound them to flatten. Combine the bread crumbs, parsley, basil and garlic powder in a soup bowl. Dredge the veal cutlets in the egg substitute in one soup bowl, dredge it in the bread crumb mixture and dry on a wire rack for 15 minutes

Sauté the cutlets in hot oil for 2 to 3 minutes on each side until browned. Drain on paper towels. Garnish with lemon slices.

Veal Scaloppini

Serves 4

1 pound thin veal cutlets
½ cup all-purpose flour
½ pound fresh mushrooms, sliced
2 tablespoons polyunsaturated oil
½ cup low salt chicken stock
½ cup dry white wine
¼ teaspoon freshly ground black pepper
1 teaspoon kosher salt
Juice of 1 lemon

Dredge the veal in the flour. In a skillet, brown the veal and mushrooms in the oil. Add the chicken stock, wine, pepper, salt and cook, covered, over low heat for 30 minutes. Add the lemon juice and cook 5 minutes more.

~~

Osso Buco

Serves 4

4 1-inch thick osso buco veal shanks
1 cup flour for dredging
½ cup extra virgin olive oil
1 white onion, thinly sliced
1 bay leaf
2 small carrots, thinly sliced in coins
1 celery rib, diced
½ cup dry white wine
2½ cups canned diced tomatoes
1 tablespoon tomato paste
2 tablespoon flat leaf parsley, coarsely chopped
1 tablespoon grated lemon zest
1 teaspoon kosher salt
½ teaspoon freshly ground black pepper

Dredge the veal shanks in flour to coat evenly. Brown in olive oil in a skillet and remove to a platter.

Add the onion, bay leaf, carrot and celery and cook over medium heat until the onion is translucent. Add the wine and simmer until the wine evaporates. Add the veal shanks, tomatoes, tomato paste and cover. Simmer for 1½ hours.

When done, remove the veal from the pan. Strain the sauce and puree the vegetables in a blender or food processor. Place the meat, the puree and the sauce in the pan, stir in the parsley, lemon zest, salt and pepper, cover and simmer for 5 minutes to blend the flavors.

~~

Veal Cacciatore

Serves 4

1 pound thin veal cutlets
½ cup all-purpose flour
1 teaspoon kosher salt
1 teaspoon freshly ground black pepper
2 tablespoons polyunsaturated oil
1 16-ounce can diced tomatoes
2 tablespoons chopped onions
12 medium mushrooms, sliced
2 cloves garlic, minced
¾ cup dry red wine
2 teaspoons oregano
2 teaspoons basil
3 tablespoons parsley

Place the veal between two layers of waxed paper and pound until ¼ inch thick. Season the veal with the salt and pepper and dredge in the flour.

In a skillet, Sauté the veal in the oil over medium heat until browned. Remove from the skillet to a platter and keep warm.

Sauté the mushrooms, onions and garlic in the same skillet for 5 minutes. Add the tomatoes, oregano, basil and parsley and simmer for 10 minutes. Return the veal to the skillet and warm the mixture. Garnish with parsley.

Sherried Veal

Serves 4

1 pound thin veal cutlets
2 tablespoons lemon juice
5 tablespoons polyunsaturated oil
2 garlic cloves, minced
1 cup low salt chicken stock
¼ cup dry sherry
Freshly ground black pepper
Kosher salt

Marinate the meat in the lemon juice and 3 tablespoons of oil for one hour. Drain.

Sauté the veal in the remaining oil until lightly browned on both sides and remove from the skillet.

Sauté the garlic in the oil that remains in the skillet until it is translucent. Add the stock and sherry and boil for 10 minutes. Add salt and pepper to taste and pour over the veal.

~~

Veal Marsala

Serves 4

1 pound thin veal cutlets
2 garlic cloves, minced
1½ teaspoons kosher salt
¼ teaspoon freshly ground black pepper
¼ teaspoon oregano
¼ teaspoon rosemary
1 cup sliced mushrooms
2 tablespoons Marsala wine

Rub the veal with the garlic and then sprinkle it with the salt and pepper and brown in a nonstick skillet. Add the remaining ingredients, cover and simmer over low heat for 15 minutes.

Wiener Schnitzel

Serves 6

12 anchovy fillets, chopped
¼ cup capers
6 4-ounce veal cutlets
1 teaspoon kosher salt
½ teaspoon freshly ground black pepper
2 cups liquid egg substitute
1 cup flour
3½ cups unflavored bread crumbs
6 tablespoons polyunsaturated margarine
6 tablespoons extra virgin olive oil
3 lemons, cut into wedges

Mix the anchovies and capers in a bowl and set aside.

Place the veal cutlets between 2 layers of plastic wrap and pound until ¼ inch thick. Sprinkle with salt and pepper. Dip each cutlet in egg substitute and then breadcrumbs to coat.

Melt 2 tablespoons of the margarine with 2 tablespoons of olive oil in a large skillet over medium high heat. Add 2 cutlets to the skillet and cook until golden brown on each side. Transfer the cooked cutlet to a dish, cover and keep warm while cooking the next 2 and then the final 2 cutlets.

Spread the anchovies and capers over the cutlets and garnish with lemon wedges.

FRAYDA FAIGEL AND HARRIS FAIGEL

Petit Syrah - Braised Veal Chops

Serves 4

2 tablespoons polyunsaturated oil
4 6-ounce shoulder veal chops, 1 inch thick
1 teaspoon kosher salt
¼ teaspoon freshly ground black pepper
10 garlic cloves, quartered
1 cup Petit Syrah red wine
⅓ cup dried cherries
⅓ cup dried plums, halved
⅓ cup dried apricots, halved
2 cups low salt beef stock
¼ teaspoon ground cinnamon
¼ teaspoon ground nutmeg
1 bay leaf
2 tablespoons fresh chives, chopped

Heat the oil in a large skillet. Season the veal chops with salt and pepper and add to the skillet together with the garlic and cook over high heat until the chops and garlic brown.

Add the wine, cherries, plums and apricots to the skillet and bring to a boil. Heat until the wine is reduced in half. Add the beef stock, cinnamon, nutmeg and bay leaf and bring to a boil. Reduce the heat to medium, cover and simmer until the veal is tender and the sauce is thickened, about 30 minutes.

Transfer the chops to a warm plate, drizzle with sauce and garnish with chives.

Chapter XII - Fish

Halibut With Shrimp And Mushrooms

Serves 6

6 6-ounce halibut fillets
1 tablespoon kosher salt
2 bay leaves
1 sweet white onion, sliced
1 teaspoon thyme
½ teaspoon celery seeds
¼ teaspoon caraway seeds
2 tablespoons extra virgin olive oil
1 clove garlic, crushed
4 tablespoons dry sherry
½ pound crimini mushrooms
1 pound medium shrimp, peeled and deveined
¼ cup polyunsaturated margarine
½ cup flour
¼ teaspoon freshly ground black pepper
¼ teaspoon onion powder
1½ cups low salt chicken stock

Poach the fish in water seasoned with the salt, bay leaves, onion, thyme, celery seeds and caraway seeds for 10 minutes. Remove the fish from the stock, drain and reserve the liquid.

Sauté the garlic in the olive oil. Add the sherry, shrimp and mushrooms and cook over low heat until the shrimp turn pink.

Melt the margarine in a pan, stir in the flour, pepper, onion powder and chicken stock until thickened. Add the mushrooms and shrimp.

Spread a thin layer of sauce in the bottom of a baking dish, lay the fish in the sauce and spread the remaining sauce over the fish. Bake at 350 degree for 15 minutes.

Clam Sauce For Pasta

Serves 6

⅓ cup polyunsaturated oil
2 large garlic cloves, minced
1 teaspoon dried basil
1 15-ounce can chopped clams, drained
¼ cup flat leaf parsley, coarsely chopped
1½ cups clam juice
½ teaspoon kosher salt
¼ teaspoon freshly ground black pepper
Pasta

In a large skillet, Sauté the garlic in the oil until just translucent. Add the basil and clams and simmer for 5 minutes. Add the parsley and clam juice and simmer for 10 minutes. Stir in the salt and pepper. Serve over hot cooked pasta.

~~

Flounder Toscano

Serves 6

2 cups water
½ teaspoon kosher salt
1½ pounds flounder fillets
1 pound frozen spinach, defrosted and drained
3 tablespoons polyunsaturated margarine
3 tablespoons flour
1¼ cups nonfat milk
¼ cup grated Parmesan cheese

Bring the water to a boil in a large skillet, add the salt and simmer the flounder in the water for 10 minutes until the fish flakes.
Melt 1 tablespoon of margarine in a baking dish, place a layer of spinach in the bottom and place the fish on top of the spinach. Melt the remaining margarine in a small sauce pan, stir in the flour and cook over medium heat until it becomes a paste. Add the milk gradually and continue stirring until the mixture thickens. Pour the sauce over the spinach, sprinkle with the cheese and broil until lightly browned.

Monkfish Salad

Serves 6

2 pounds cooked firm monkfish
1 16-ounce can diced tomatoes, drained
4 tablespoons chili sauce
½ cup Greek yogurt
¼ cup diced pimientos
¼ cup diced green pepper
¼ cup diced celery
¼ teaspoon paprika
Whole pitted green olives
Whole pitted black olives

Mix together all the ingredients except for the olives and place in a serving bowl. Garnish the salad with the olives.

~~

Langostinos Bourguignon

Serves 6

2 pounds frozen langostinos
1 cup dry red wine
1 teaspoon kosher salt
½ teaspoon thyme
¼ cup finely chopped flat leaf parsley
4 shallots, minced
4 cloves garlic, minced
6 ounces polyunsaturated margarine
2 ounces toasted sesame seeds

Season the langostinos with salt, thyme, 1 minced garlic clove and 1 tablespoon parsley and poach in the red wine for 2 minutes. Remove the langostinos from the liquid and rinse under cold water to stop the cooking.

Cream the margarine with the remaining garlic, the shallots and ⅔ of the remaining parsley.

Place the cooled langostinos in 6 ramekins. Top each ramekin with the margarine and sprinkle with sesame seeds. Broil for 2-4 minutes until the tops brown well.

Salmon Croquettes

Serves 4

1 16-ounce can pink or red salmon
1 tablespoon finely chopped onion
¾ cup seasoned Italian breadcrumbs
¼ teaspoon kosher salt
¼ teaspoon freshly ground black pepper
1 tablespoon Dijon mustard
1 tablespoon Old Bay seasoning
⅛ teaspoon cayenne pepper
¼ cup liquid egg substitute
3 tablespoons nonfat milk
Polyunsaturated oil

Drain liquid from the salmon. Reserve. In a bowl place the salmon, onion, breadcrumbs, salt, and pepper and mix well.

Add the liquid egg substitute, liquid from the salmon and the milk. Add the mustard, Old Bay seasoning and cayenne pepper. Mix well and form into six patties and roll in the breadcrumbs. Sauté in the oil until brown on both sides.

For tuna croquettes, used 3 5-ounce cans of tuna in place of salmon.

~~

Salmon Steaks

Serves 4

4 salmon steaks, 1 inch thick
4 teaspoons polyunsaturated margarine
4 teaspoons flat leaf parsley, chopped
2 teaspoons freshly squeezed lemon juice
Lemon wedges
Fresh whole flat leaf parsley

Place 1 teaspoon margarine on top of each salmon steak. Sprinkle each steak with 1 teaspoon chopped parsley and ½ teaspoon lemon juice.

Broil for 15 minutes. Garnish with a sprig of fresh parsley and a lemon wedge.

Sweet Potato Crusted Flounder

Serves 4

2 medium sweet potatoes
4 6-ounce flounder fillets
½ teaspoon kosher salt
¼ teaspoon freshly ground white pepper
¼ cup Dijon mustard
1 lemon, quartered
¼ cup flat leaf parsley, chopped

Bake the sweet potatoes for 30 minutes, cool and mash. Add the salt, pepper and mustard and mix well. Place the flounder in a square baking dish and coat with the sweet potato mixture. Broil the fish for 15 minutes or until the potato crust is browned. Garnish with lemon and parsley.

~~

Garlic Lemon Shrimp

Serves 6

½ cup dry white wine
2 tablespoons white vinegar
8 large garlic cloves, minced
2 tablespoons fresh rosemary, minced
1 stick polyunsaturated margarine, cut into small pieces
2 tablespoons freshly squeezed Meyer lemon juice
2 tablespoons polyunsaturated oil
2 pounds uncooked large shrimp, peeled and deveined
½ teaspoon kosher salt
2 tablespoons chopped fresh chives

Bring the white wine, vinegar, rosemary and garlic to a boil in a small pan and cook until reduced in half. Reduce the heat to low and whisk in the margarine, melting 1 piece at a time. Stir in the lemon juice and remove from the heat.

In a large skillet, heat the polyunsaturated oil over high heat until the surface glistens. Add the shrimp and sauté until they turn pink (about 2-3 minutes). Place the shrimp on plates, sprinkle with salt and spread the lemon-garlic over each one. Garnish with chives.

Garlic Sea Scallops

Serves 4

½ stick polyunsaturated margarine
8 fresh shiitake mushrooms, stemmed and thinly sliced
3 garlic cloves, minced
1 teaspoon onion powder
¼ cup low salt soy sauce
4 tablespoons dry white wine
6 drops Tabasco sauce
12 sea scallops
1 teaspoon kosher salt
½ teaspoon freshly ground black pepper

Melt 2 tablespoons of margarine in a skillet over medium heat, add the mushrooms and garlic and sauté for 5 minutes. Add the onion powder and stir. Add the soy sauce, wine and Tabasco and simmer until the sauce begins to thicken.
Melt the remaining margarine in a skillet over medium high heat. Season the scallops with the salt and pepper, add the scallops to the skillet and sauté for 3 minutes. Add the sauce, reduce the heat and simmer for 2 minutes more.

~~

Baked Stuffed Tilapia

Serves 6

2 pounds fresh or frozen tilapia fillets
¼ teaspoon kosher salt
¼ teaspoon freshly ground black pepper
¼ teaspoon garlic powder
1 tablespoon minced red onion
3 cups bread crumbs
6 tablespoons polyunsaturated margarine, melted

Mix together the salt, pepper, garlic powder, onion bread crumbs and half the margarine until moist.
Place a layer of half of the fish in a glass baking dish, cover with the breadcrumb mixture. Place the remaining fish on top of the breadcrumbs and brush the fish with the remaining margarine.
Bake at 350 degrees for 30 minutes.

Scallops And Shrimp In White Bean Sauce

Serves 4

¼ cup sweet red onion, finely chopped
1 large garlic clove, minced
2 tablespoons polyunsaturated oil
¼ cup dry white wine
¼ cup fresh basil
¼ cup fresh flat leaf parsley
1 cup cannellini beans, drained and rinsed
¼ cup bottled clam juice
¼ teaspoon kosher salt
¼ pound bay scallops
½ pound medium uncooked shrimp, peeled and deveined
Linguini

Cook the onion and garlic in one tablespoon of oil in a small saucepan over low heat until the onion is soft. Add the wine, increase the heat to medium and simmer until the mixture is reduce in half. Add the basil, parsley, ½ cup of beans and the clam juice and simmer. Puree this mixture in a blender. Return the puree to the saucepan, add the remaining beans and salt and keep warm.

Heat the remaining oil in a skillet over high heat and then sauté the scallops and the shrimp until the shrimp are pink and the scallops no longer translucent.

Mix the scallops and shrimp with the bean sauce and serve over linguini.

~~

Tuna Casserole

Serves 4

1 can condensed cream of potato soup
⅓ cup nonfat milk
1 can dark tuna, packed in oil, drained and flaked
2 hard-boiled eggs, sliced
1 can white beans
1½ cups crumbled potato chips

Blend the soup and milk in a 1 quart casserole dish. Stir in the tuna, eggs and beans. Bake for 20 minutes at 350 degrees. Cover the tuna with the potato chips and bake for another 10 minutes.

Sole Newburg

Serves 4

1 pound fillets of sole
½ teaspoon kosher salt
¼ teaspoon mace
¼ teaspoon freshly ground black pepper
¼ cup extra virgin olive oil
½ cup all-purpose flour
¾ cup evaporated nonfat milk
¼ cup liquid egg substitute
3 tablespoon dry sherry

Place the fish fillets in a baking dish sprayed with nonstick olive oil spray. Mix the salt, mace, pepper and olive oil and spread over the fish. Bake for 30 minutes at 350 degrees.

Blend the flour with the milk in a saucepan with a whisk, stirring constantly over medium heat until thickened. Add half of the hot mixture to the liquid egg substitute and blend. Combine with the rest of the mixture. Heat until steaming and add the sherry. Cook for 5 minutes and pour over the fish.

~~

Shrimp And Chickpeas Niçoise

Serves 4

1 pound large raw shrimp, shelled and deveined
½ 15-ounce can of chickpeas, rinsed and drained
3 large garlic cloves
¼ teaspoon chili flakes
¼ cup flat leaf parsley
¼ cup fresh basil
¼ teaspoon ground coriander
½ teaspoon sweet paprika
1½ teaspoons extra virgin olive oil
½ teaspoon kosher salt
¼ teaspoon freshly ground black pepper
1 medium red onion, coarsely diced
1 can whole tomatoes with juice
1 lemon cut into 8 wedges

In a food processor, mince together the garlic, parsley, basil, coriander and paprika with 1½ tablespoons olive oil. Place the shrimp in one bowl, the chickpeas in a second, divide the herb mixture between them and refrigerate for 20-30 minutes.

Coat a sauté pan with non stick spray and sauté the shrimp and seasonings over high heat until beginning to turn pink and remove from the pan. Spray the pan again, brown the onion and then stir in the chickpeas with their seasonings and sauté over medium heat for 5 minutes. Break the tomatoes with a fork and add them with their liquid to the chickpeas. Cook, stirring for 5 minutes. Stir in the shrimp. Serve garnished with lemon wedges.

~~

Baked Bay Scallops

Serves 4

¼ stick polyunsaturated margarine
¾ pound bay scallops
½ teaspoon kosher salt
¼ teaspoon freshly ground black pepper
1 cup unflavored fresh bread crumbs
2 large garlic cloves, crushed
3 tablespoons freshly chopped flat leaf parsley
½ teaspoon tarragon
½ teaspoon thyme
1 lemon

Melt the margarine in the microwave and brush a little on the bottom of a glass pie dish. Place the scallops in the dish in a single layer and sprinkle with salt and pepper. Add the bread crumbs to the remaining melted margarine and stir in the garlic, parsley, tarragon and thyme and sauté until the bread crumbs become crisp. Spread the flavored bread crumbs over the scallops and bake at 450 degrees for 10 minutes. Garnish with lemon wedges.

Gravlax

Serves 8

½ cup kosher salt
½ cup granulated sugar
¼ teaspoon freshly ground white pepper
2 bunches fresh dill
3 tablespoons vodka
2 pounds salmon fillets, center cut

Rinse the salmon in cold water, pat dry and remove any remaining pin bones.

Combine the salt, sugar, pepper and vodka in a bowl and mix thoroughly.

Line a glass baking dish with enough plastic wrap to permit folding over the entire dish. Place one bunch of dill in a layer in the bottom of the dish. Place the salmon on the dill with the skin side down and press the salt/sugar mixture over the entire surface. Place the remaining bunch of dill in a layer on top of the salmon and wrap the salmon tightly in the plastic wrap. Place a heavy weight (a brick or two wrapped in aluminum foil that covers the salmon will do) and refrigerate for 1 week.

Remove the gravlax from the plastic wrap and the dill and wash off the salt/sugar mixture. Rewrap the salmon in fresh plastic tightly and refrigerate for one week before serving.

~~

Grilled Halibut With Green Olives

Serves 4

1 tablespoon freshly squeezed lime juice
¼ cup plus 1 tablespoon freshly squeezed orange juice
1 tablespoon minced fresh ginger
1 tablespoon minced garlic
¼ tablespoon allspice
¼ tablespoon caraway seeds, crushed
1¼ teaspoon freshly ground black pepper
1½ tablespoons molasses
¼ cup Southern Comfort
4 ½-inch thick halibut fillets or steaks
1½ teaspoons Dijon mustard
2 teaspoons red wine vinegar

½ cup extra virgin olive oil
1 cup pitted whole green olives
½ teaspoon kosher salt
Leafy green lettuce

Mix the lime juice, 1 tablespoon orange juice, ginger, garlic, allspice, caraway seeds, 1 tablespoon black pepper, molasses and Southern Comfort. Dredge the halibut in the marinade, Wrap the fish in plastic wrap and refrigerate.

Mix the ¼ cup orange juice, mustard and vinegar in a bowl and whisk in the olive oil.

In a frying pan, grill the halibut for 3 minutes on each side, basting with the sauce. Add the green olives, remaining pepper and serve over a leafy green lettuce.

~~

Mussels Dijon

Serves 4

6 ounces extra virgin olive oil
½ cup shallots, diced
6 large garlic cloves
1 tablespoon dry thyme
½ teaspoon kosher salt
¼ teaspoon freshly ground white pepper
⅓ cup Dijon mustard
2 cups dry white wine
4 pounds mussels
¼ cup minced flat leaf parsley

Warm the olive oil in a large pot over medium heat. Add the shallots, garlic, thyme, salt and white pepper, lower the heat and cook gently for 2 minutes. Add the mustard and wine and bring to a boil. Then reduce the heat and simmer for 5 minutes. Increase the heat, bring the broth to a boil and add the mussels, stir, cover and cook until all the mussels have opened.

Tilapia Provençale

Serves 4

2 tablespoons polyunsaturated oil
2 tomatoes, diced
1 large onion, diced
4 tilapia fillets
1 teaspoon dry oregano
½ teaspoon kosher salt
¼ teaspoon freshly ground white pepper
¼ teaspoon Worcestershire sauce

Heat the oil in an ovenproof skillet, add the tomato and onion and sauté until tender. Remove the tomato and onion from the skillet and add the Worcestershire sauce. Place the tilapia in the skillet and sprinkle with the oregano, salt and pepper. Spoon the tomato and onion mixture over the fish and bake at 350 degrees for 15 minutes.

~~

Oven-Fried Tilapia Fillet

Serves 4

1 pound tilapia fillets
1 cup bread crumbs
¼ cup grape nuts cereal, crushed
½ cup shredded Asiago cheese
¼ cup French dressing
2 teaspoons polyunsaturated oil

Preheat the oven to 500 degrees.

Mix the bread crumbs, grape nuts cereal and cheese. Dredge the fish in the French dressing and then in the bread crumb mixture. Arrange the fish on an oiled baking pan and pour any remaining French dressing and bread crumbs over the fish. Bake for 12 minutes until fish flakes easily with a fork.

Flounder Romano

Serves 4

1 pound flounder fillets
2 tablespoons polyunsaturated oil
1 onion, chopped
2 tablespoons flat leaf parsley, chopped
1 8-ounce can diced tomatoes with juice
½ teaspoon kosher salt
½ teaspoon basil
½ teaspoon oregano
¼ teaspoon freshly ground black pepper
½ cup grated Romano cheese

Heat the oil in a skillet. Add the onion and parsley and sauté over medium heat until the onion is translucent. Add the tomatoes and seasonings and cook for 10 minutes. Add the fish, cover and simmer for 10 minutes until the fish flakes easily. Sprinkle with the cheese before serving.

~~

Trout In White Wine Sauce

Serves 6

½ cup scallions, diced
⅔ cup dry white wine
2 garlic cloves, crushed
1½ teaspoons kosher salt
¼ teaspoon freshly ground black pepper
1 teaspoon Worcestershire sauce
½ cup water
6 fresh trout
Lemon wedges and whole scallions for garnish

In a 12-inch nonstick skillet over high heat, bring the scallions, wine, garlic, salt, pepper, Worcestershire and water to a boil. Add the trout, reduce the heat to low, cover and simmer for 8 to 10 minutes until the fish flakes. Place the fish on a warm platter and garnish with lemon and scallions.

Rolled Fillet Of Sole In White Wine Sauce

Serves 4

1½ pounds fillet of sole
½ teaspoon kosher salt
¼ teaspoon freshly ground black pepper
¼ teaspoon thyme
¼ teaspoon tarragon
4 tablespoons polyunsaturated margarine
2 tablespoons minced shallots
½ pound brown mushrooms, thinly sliced
½ cup dry white wine
2 tablespoons freshly squeezed lemon juice
Lemon wedges
Flat leaf parsley sprigs

Combine the salt, pepper, thyme and tarragon. Rub over the fish fillets and set aside.

Melt 2 tablespoons of margarine, add the shallots and mushrooms and cook for 3 minutes over medium heat. Lay the fish fillets on a flat surface, spread with the shallot and mushroom mixture, roll and secure with toothpicks.

Place the rolled fillets in a skillet. Melt the remaining margarine, stir in the wine and lemon juice and pour over the fish. Simmer gently for 15 minutes until the fish flakes.

Serve garnished with lemon wedges and parsley sprigs.

~~

Tomato Shrimp

Serves 4

¼ cup polyunsaturated oil
3 medium shallots, chopped
1 pound uncooked medium shrimp, peeled and deveined
1 tablespoon tomato paste
⅓ cup dry white wine
¼ teaspoon crushed red pepper
6 large plum tomatoes, coarsely chopped
½ cup pitted Kalamata olives
4 large garlic cloves, finely minced
½ cup condensed skim milk
½ teaspoon kosher salt
¼ teaspoon freshly ground white pepper

¼ cup fresh basil, coarsely chopped
Linguini

In a large skillet, heat the oil over medium heat and sauté the shallots until translucent. Add the shrimp and cook until turning pink. Transfer the shrimp to a bowl, add the tomato paste to skillet and stir. Add the wine, crushed red pepper and bring to a boil for 2 minutes. Add the tomatoes, olives and garlic and cook until the sauce begins to thicken. Add the condensed skim milk, salt and pepper and simmer. Serve over linguini garnished with the fresh basil.

~~

Roasted Cod

Serves 6

1 tablespoon extra virgin olive oil
1 pint cherry tomatoes
½ teaspoon kosher salt
¼ teaspoon freshly ground black pepper
2 teaspoons polyunsaturated margarine
1½ pounds cod, boneless and skinless, cut into 6 pieces
½ cup dry white wine
1 teaspoon dried tarragon
1 lemon, quartered

Heat the oil over medium heat in a large skillet. Add the tomatoes, salt and pepper and cook, stirring for 3 minutes. Add the fish and cook for 2 more minutes. Pour in the wine, top each piece of fish with ½ teaspoon margarine and tarragon. Cover the pan and roast in a 350 degree oven for 8 minutes until the fish is cooked and the tomatoes begin to burst. Serve with the sauce and lemon quarters.

Broiled Halibut

Serves 6

2 pounds halibut steaks
2 teaspoons polyunsaturated oil
2 teaspoons polyunsaturated margarine, melted
¼ teaspoon kosher salt
¼ teaspoon freshly ground black pepper
¼ teaspoon paprika
2 tablespoons lemon juice
1 lemon cut into wedges
1 tablespoon flat leaf parsley, chopped

Arrange the fish on an oiled broiling pan. Mix the melted margarine, salt, pepper, paprika and lemon juice and brush on the fish steaks. Broil on one side for 10 minutes until the halibut flakes easily with a fork. Garnish with lemon wedges and parsley.

~~

Barbequed Swordfish Niçoise

Serves 4

8 ounces caponata (see recipe on page 67)
¾ cup whole pitted green olives
¼ cup oil-cured pitted black olives
2 anchovy fillets
1 tablespoon white wine vinegar
1 large garlic clove, minced
½ teaspoon dry thyme
¼ teaspoon kosher salt
¼ teaspoon freshly ground white pepper
4 6-ounce swordfish steaks
2 tablespoon extra virgin olive oil
¼ cup fresh flat leaf parsley
1 lemon, quartered

Combine the caponata, green olives, black olives, anchovy, vinegar, garlic, thyme, salt and pepper in a bowl.

On a hot grill, coat the swordfish with olive oil and barbeque the fish for 3 minutes per side. Stir the parsley into the caponata mixture and arrange on top of the fish. Garnish with lemon wedges.

Scallops En Brochette

Serves 6

2 pounds fresh sea scallops
½ cup liquid egg substitute
2 tablespoons bacon substitute, ground

Thread the scallops onto skewers and dip into the egg substitute. Sprinkle with the ground bacon substitute. Broil until browned.

~~

Crabmeat Pie

Serves 6

1 10-inch pie crust
¼ pound St. Otho cheese
¼ cup Asiago cheese
½ cup 31-40 small shrimp
½ cup crabmeat
¼ cup mushrooms, chopped
½ cup liquid egg substitute
1 tablespoon flour
⅔ cup nonfat milk
¼ teaspoon kosher salt
¼ teaspoon freshly ground black pepper
¼ teaspoon cayenne
¼ teaspoon freshly ground nutmeg
2 tablespoons dry sherry
2 tablespoons polyunsaturated oil

In the bottom of the pie crust, layer the cheeses, then the shrimp, the crabmeat and then the mushrooms.

Combine the egg substitute, milk, flour, salt, pepper, cayenne and nutmeg. Stir in the sherry and oil and mix well. Pour over the crab, shrimp and mushrooms. Bake at 375 degrees for 40 minutes or until browned. Cool for 20 minutes before serving.

Lime-Glazed Swordfish

Serves 2

¼ cup freshly squeezed lime juice
¼ cup honey
1½ tablespoons low salt soy sauce
1 teaspoon minced fresh ginger
1 tablespoon extra virgin olive oil
1 teaspoon garlic powder
½ teaspoon lime zest
2 6-ounce swordfish belly fillets
1 lime, cut into quarters

Whisk the lime juice, honey, soy sauce, ginger, olive oil, garlic powder and zest in a large bowl. Add the swordfish to the marinade and refrigerate for 3 hours. Remove the swordfish from the marinade. In a small saucepan, bring the marinade to a boil and reduce in half. Place the swordfish on a pan lined with aluminum foil and broil for 3 minutes per side. Spoon the glaze over the swordfish and broil for 2 minutes more. Garnish with lime wedges.

~~

Macaroni Tuna

Serves 6

1 cup elbow macaroni
2 tablespoon extra virgin olive oil
2 tablespoon red wine vinegar
2 tablespoons water
½ teaspoon kosher salt
½ teaspoon dry basil
½ teaspoon dry oregano
½ teaspoon garlic powder
½ teaspoon Dijon mustard
2 cans dark tuna packed in water, drained and flaked
½ cup chopped celery
½ cup sweet red pepper, seeded and chopped
½ cup canned diced tomatoes, drained
3 tablespoons mayonnaise
Soft-leaf lettuce

Bring 1 quart of water to a boil in a large pot. Add the macaroni and cook stirring occasionally until *al dente*, about 8 minutes. Drain and rinse.

Combine the oil, vinegar, water, salt, basil, oregano, garlic powder and mustard in a skillet and heat until steaming. Add the tuna, celery, diced tomatoes and red pepper, toss and chill. Stir in the mayonnaise and serve on soft-leaf lettuce.

~~

Pan-Roasted Salmon

Serves 6

2 pounds center-cut salmon fillets
1 tablespoon polyunsaturated margarine
1 tablespoon extra virgin olive oil
½ teaspoon kosher salt
¼ teaspoon freshly ground black pepper
½ medium red pepper, diced
4 tablespoons dry white wine
1 lemon, cut into wedges

Rinse and pat the salmon dry. Remove any small remaining pin bones.

Heat the margarine and olive oil in a large sauté pan. Salt and pepper the fish and place it in the pan skin down. Sear for 2 minutes over high heat. Carefully turn the fish over and sear for 2 minutes on the second side. Spread the onions around the fish, reduce the heat to low, cover the pan and cook for 3 minutes. Turn the fish over, cover again and cook for 3 more minutes and remove from the pan. Return the pan to high heat and sauté the onions until limp. Add the wine, scrape up the brown bits in the pan and pour the juices and sauce over the fish.

Portuguese Steamed Clams

Serves 4

2 tablespoons polyunsaturated oil
1 pound hot Italian sausage
½ cup shallots, chopped
4 garlic cloves, diced
½ teaspoon crushed red pepper flakes
1 large can diced tomatoes in juice
1 cup low salt chicken stock
2 tablespoons balsamic vinegar
4 pounds littleneck clams
½ cup fresh basil, coarsely chopped

Heat the olive oil in a large pot. Add the sausage, sauté until cooked through, breaking up with a fork. Add the shallots, garlic and pepper flakes and stir well. Pour off the excess fat. Mix in the tomatoes and juices, chicken stock and vinegar. Add the clams, bring to a boil and cook until all the clams open. Mix in the basil.

~~

Tuna Steaks With Horseradish Sauce

Serves 4

4 6-ounce tuna steaks
2 tablespoons polyunsaturated oil
1 teaspoon kosher salt
½ teaspoon freshly ground white pepper
1 lemon, cut into quarters
3 tablespoons freshly ground horseradish
3 tablespoons polyunsaturated margarine
½ teaspoon kosher salt
¼ teaspoon freshly ground black pepper
½ teaspoon granulated sugar
½ teaspoon white wine vinegar

Heat a heavy skillet over medium high heat. Coat the tuna with oil, salt and pepper and sear for 4 minutes per side. Increase heat to high and sear each side for 3-4 minutes more until a crust forms.

Mix the horseradish, margarine, salt, pepper and sugar into a paste and then mix in the vinegar. Spread the sauce over the tuna just before serving.

Scrod With Capers And Roasted Tomatoes

Serves 4

4 4-ounce scrod fillets
¼ teaspoon freshly ground black pepper
1 16-ounce can diced tomatoes, drained
½ teaspoon kosher salt
½ cup pitted black olives
1 tablespoon capers
2 tablespoons dry white wine
1 lemon cut into quarters

Remove any small bones from the fish, place in a medium casserole and sprinkle with the pepper. Spread the diced tomatoes in a glass dish, mix in the salt and broil for 10 minutes. Pour the broiled diced tomatoes over the fish, top each piece with capers and olives and sprinkle with white wine. Bake uncovered for 20 minutes. Garnish with lemon wedges.

~~

Potato Crusted Cod

Serves 4

4 baking potatoes, peeled and cut into 1-inch cubes
1 teaspoon kosher salt
1 quart water
½ teaspoon freshly ground black pepper
4 teaspoons extra virgin olive oil
4 cloves garlic, minced
4 6-ounce cod fillets
2 teaspoons polyunsaturated oil

Boil the potatoes in a medium saucepan in 1 quart of salted water for 15 minutes, drain and place in a large bowl. Add the salt and pepper, olive oil, garlic and milk while mashing until thoroughly mixed. Coat the cod fillets with oil, place in a roasting pan, spread with the potatoes. Roast at 450 degrees for 10 minutes.

Broiled Scrod

Serves 4

1 pound scrod fillets
½ cup saltine cracker crumbs
½ cup corn flakes, crushed
½ cup sapsago cheese, grated
1 tablespoon polyunsaturated margarine
½ teaspoon paprika

Lay the fillets in a baking dish lightly greased with the margarine. Sprinkle the fish with the cheese, breadcrumbs and paprika and dot with margarine. Bake at 400 degrees for 15 minutes. Raise the fish to the broiling shelf and broil until the top is golden brown.

~~

Tuna Stuffed Portabella Mushrooms

Serves 4

1 can dark tuna in oil
2 tablespoons sweet red pepper, finely diced
2 tablespoons celery, finely diced
½ teaspoon red pepper flakes
6 anchovies, mashed
1 tablespoon pitted black olives, finely diced
1 clove garlic, finely diced
2 tablespoons low fat plain yogurt
½ teaspoon kosher salt
2 tablespoons feta cheese, crumbled
4 large portabella mushrooms

Drain the tuna and reserve the oil. Place the tuna in a bowl and break it into loose flakes. Add the sweet pepper, celery, red pepper flakes, anchovies, olives, garlic, 1 tablespoon of the tuna oil, yogurt and salt and mix well. Divide the tuna into four portions and spoon into the mushroom caps. Sprinkle each mushroom with feta cheese and bake at 350 degrees for 20 minutes until the cheese begins to brown.

Fish Kabobs

Serves 8

2 pounds perch, halibut, cod or trout
⅓ cup polyunsaturated oil
½ cup freshly squeezed lemon juice
1 tablespoon oregano
¼ teaspoon freshly ground black pepper
5 bay leaves
3 medium onions, quartered
2 tomatoes, quartered
8 mushroom caps

Cut the fish into 8 pieces and place in a deep bowl. Blend the oil, oregano and pepper and pour over the fish and bay leaves. Marinate at room temperature for 3 hours.

Skewer the fish on one skewer. Skewer the onions, tomatoes and mushroom caps on a second skewer. Broil the vegetables for 10 minutes. Add the fish skewer to the broiler and continue to broil for 7 minutes more.

~~

Baked Shrimp

Serves 6

2 pounds raw shrimp, peeled and deveined
¼ pound polyunsaturated margarine, melted
1 teaspoon Dijon mustard
4 cloves garlic
½ teaspoon chili powder
2 tablespoons freshly squeezed lemon juice
¼ teaspoon kosher salt
¼ teaspoon freshly ground black pepper
2 tablespoons dry white wine

Mix all the ingredients together in a bowl, cover with clear plastic wrap and refrigerate for 24 hours. Drain the shrimp. reserve the liquid. Place shrimp in a flat baking dish. Bake at 350 degrees for 10 minutes, basting regularly with the reserved liquid. Then broil briefly until the tails turn brown.

Baked Stuffed Snapper

Serves 6

1 4 to 5 pound whole snapper
1 teaspoon kosher salt
4 cups breadcrumbs
½ stick polyunsaturated margarine
1 medium yellow onion, finely chopped
1 pound white mushrooms, chopped
¼ cup flat leaf parsley, chopped
½ teaspoon basil
4 teaspoons freshly squeezed orange juice
¼ teaspoon marjoram
¼ teaspoon thyme
2 tablespoons extra virgin olive oil
Lemon wedges

Sprinkle the fish with salt inside and out.

Melt the margarine in a skillet. Add the onions and mushrooms and cook until tender. Add the parsley, basil, orange juice, marjoram and thyme and mix. Add the breadcrumbs and mix well. Stuff the fish with the breadcrumb mixture, brush with olive oil and bake at 350 degrees for 45 minutes in a pan sprayed with nonstick spray.

Garnish with lemon wedges.

~~

Tuna Tetrazzini

Serves 4

4 tablespoons polyunsaturated margarine
1 pound white mushrooms, thinly sliced
1 8-ounce package linguine
¼ cup all-purpose flour
1½ cups nonfat milk
3 tablespoons dry sherry
8 ounces Asiago cheese, cut in small pieces
¼ teaspoon allspice
¼ teaspoon thyme
1 7-ounce can Italian Tonno in oil, drained

Melt half the margarine in a skillet, add the mushrooms and sauté until softened.

In a saucepan, cook the linguine according to the directions until *al dente*. Drain and set aside.

In a large saucepan, melt the remaining margarine and stir in the flour until blended. Add the milk gradually, stirring continually. Add the sherry and simmer until thickened. Add the cheese and allspice and stir until the cheese is melted. Add the tuna and the mushroom mixture and serve over the linguine.

~~

Tuna a la Basque

Serves 6

2 onions, chopped
1 green pepper, seeded and chopped
1 sweet red pepper, seeded and chopped
4 tomatoes, chopped
1 pound brown mushrooms, sliced
2 tablespoons extra virgin olive oil
1 tablespoon tomato paste
½ teaspoon kosher salt
½ teaspoon freshly ground black pepper
2 garlic cloves
¼ teaspoon thyme
1 bay leaf
¼ teaspoon tarragon
¼ teaspoon marjoram
3 cans dark tuna, packed in water, drained
Brown rice

In a saucepan, sauté the onion, peppers, tomatoes and mushrooms in the olive oil. Add all the seasonings, mix well and simmer uncovered until the vegetables are soft, about 30 minutes. Add the tuna and stir until thoroughly heated.

Serve over brown rice.

Flounder Fillets In Wine And Herb Sauce

Serves 4

¾ cup dry red wine
1 tablespoon red wine vinegar
2 bay leaves
½ teaspoon rosemary
½ teaspoon onion powder
¼ teaspoon lemon thyme
4 tablespoons tomato paste
1 pound flounder fillets
¾ cup all-purpose flour
⅓ cup polyunsaturated oil
1 garlic clove, minced

Combine the wine, vinegar, bay leaves, onion powder, lemon thyme, rosemary and tomato paste and set aside.

Coat the fish with flour and sauté in hot oil until both sides are crisp and browned. Remove the fish and place on paper towels to absorb excess oil.

Sauté the garlic in the drippings wine mixture and bring to a boil. Reduce heat and simmer until thickened. Serve the fish topped with the sauce.

~~

Salmon Loaf

Serves 4

1 16 ounce can sockeye salmon
Whites of 3 eggs, beaten
¼ cup nonfat milk
½ cup flavored bread crumbs
½ large sweet onion, finely diced
1 teaspoon freshly squeezed lemon juice
½ teaspoon Dijon mustard
1 tablespoon chili sauce
1 teaspoon flat leaf parsley, coarsely chopped
½ teaspoon kosher salt
¼ teaspoon freshly ground white pepper

Combine all the ingredients in a large bowl and place in a 5 x 9 loaf pan. Bake at 350 degrees for 50 minutes.

Salmon In Mushroom Sauce

Serves 4

4 6-ounce salmon fillets
½ pound mixed wild mushrooms, coarsely chopped
1 cup dry white wine
1½ cups nonfat milk
½ teaspoon kosher salt
¼ teaspoon freshly ground white pepper

Poach the salmon and mushrooms at medium high heat in the wine for 5 minutes. Remove the salmon from the pan, add the milk, salt and pepper and increase the heat and reduce the stock until it thickens. Serve the sauce over the salmon.

~~

Trout With Orange Relish

Serves 4

1 large navel orange
4 tablespoons chopped fresh mint
2 tablespoons extra virgin olive oil
½ cup chopped Vidalia onion
2 tablespoons white wine vinegar
2 tablespoons cornmeal
1 teaspoon kosher salt
½ teaspoon freshly ground black pepper
1 2-pound trout, boned and filleted

Grate 1½ teaspoon zest from the orange. Peel the orange and discard the rest of the rind. Cut the orange into ½ inch pieces. Place in a small bowl and mix the orange zest, orange pieces and mint together.

Heat the oil in a skillet until it glistens. Sauté the onion until translucent and add the vinegar, tossing thoroughly and then add to the mixture.

Coat the fish with cornmeal, salt and pepper and sauté in the pan with the mixture. Cook for 4 minutes per side. Garnish the fish with the mixture.

[151]

Sea Scallops St. Tropez

Serves 4

1 pound sea scallops
3 tablespoons polyunsaturated oil
2 garlic cloves, coarsely chopped
2 sun-dried tomatoes in oil, drained and diced
⅛ teaspoon thyme
½ teaspoon kosher salt
¼ teaspoon freshly ground black pepper
¼ cup fresh basil, chopped
¼ cup black olives, sliced

In a skillet, sear the scallops in 1 tablespoon of oil over high heat for 2 minutes on each side until they are golden brown. Remove the scallops to a dish and cover with foil to keep warm.

Cook the garlic over medium heat in the remaining oil until translucent. Add the tomatoes and thyme and cook, stirring for 1 minute. Add the salt and pepper and stir well. Spoon the sauce over the scallops and garnish with basil and black olives.

~~

Portuguese Shellfish And Pork Stew Ribetajana

Serves 8

3 pounds boneless lean pork shoulder, cut into 1-inch pieces
2 cups dry red wine
2 tablespoon minced garlic
1 teaspoon crushed red pepper
1 teaspoon paprika
1 teaspoon kosher salt
2 8-ounce cans tomato sauce
18 large uncooked shrimp, peeled and deveined
12 fresh littleneck clams in shells
⅓ cup Kalamata olives
½ cup fresh flat leaf parsley

Combine the pork shoulder, red wine, garlic and red pepper in a bowl and refrigerate, preferably overnight.

Place the pork and marinade in a large saucepan. Add the paprika and salt, bring the pan to a boil, reduce the heat and simmer for 1½ hours. Add the tomato sauce, shrimp and clams, cover and cook over medium high heat until all the clams are open.

Garnish with olives and parsley.

~~

Pickled Shrimp

Serves 6

1¼ cups polyunsaturated oil
¾ cup white vinegar
1½ teaspoons kosher salt
2½ teaspoons celery seeds
⅛ teaspoon Tabasco
2 tablespoons freshly squeezed lemon juice
2 teaspoons minced onions
2 pounds cooked shrimp, peeled and deveined

Combine all the ingredients with the shrimp and marinate in the refrigerator for 24 hours. Serve cold.

~~

Tilapia With Mushrooms

Serves 6

¼ cup shallots, chopped
1 pound brown mushrooms, sliced
2 tablespoons polyunsaturated margarine
2 pounds tilapia fillets
2 tablespoons freshly squeezed lime juice
1 tablespoon chopped flat leaf parsley
1 teaspoon basil
¼ teaspoon freshly ground black pepper
1 teaspoon oregano
2 tablespoons dry white wine

In a large skillet, Sauté the shallots and mushrooms in the margarine until tender. Lay the tilapia in the skillet and sprinkle the remaining ingredients over the fish. Cover and simmer for 20 minutes.

[153]

Tuna Creole

Serves 6

½ cup chopped onion
½ cup chopped celery
½ cup diced green pepper
2 garlic cloves, minced
¼ cup polyunsaturated oil
1 8-ounce can tomato sauce
1 cup stewed tomatoes
¼ teaspoon chili powder
¼ teaspoon cayenne
1 teaspoon kosher salt
¼ teaspoon freshly ground black pepper
3 cans dark tuna packed in water, drained and flaked
4 cups cooked rice

Sauté the vegetables in the oil. Mix in the tomato sauce, stewed tomatoes and seasonings and simmer for 15 minutes. Add the tuna and heat thoroughly. Serve over rice.

~~

Tuna Sauce For Pasta

Serves 4

3 ounces extra virgin olive oil
1 large sweet onion, finely chopped
1 can anchovy fillets, rinsed and finely chopped
3 garlic cloves, minced
6 tablespoons fresh flat leaf parsley, coarsely chopped
1 can Italian tuna in olive oil, drained and broken into flakes
2 tablespoons capers
1 cup canned crushed tomatoes
¼ teaspoon freshly ground black pepper

In a sauté pan, warm the olive oil over medium heat and sauté the onion until translucent. Add the anchovies, garlic and parsley and cook for 1 minute. Add the tuna, capers, tomatoes and pepper and continue to cook until the sauce is warm.

Chapter XIII - Poultry

Hawaiian Chicken Jubilee

Serves 6

4 canned pineapple slices, juice reserved
½ cup chopped Canadian bacon
2 tablespoons polyunsaturated margarine
1 tablespoon chopped onions
¼ cup minced ginger
1 cup bread crumbs
6 large boneless and skinless chicken breasts
¼ cup polyunsaturated margarine
¾ cup chicken stock
2 tablespoons white wine vinegar
1 tablespoon cornstarch
½ teaspoon kosher salt
1 large can pitted sweet cherries, drained
¼ cup brandy

Dice 4 pineapple slices and sauté with the Canadian bacon in 2 tablespoons of polyunsaturated margarine. Add the onions, ginger and bread crumbs and mix well.

Place the chicken between 2 layers of plastic wrap and flatten. Spoon the stuffing into the boned side of the chicken, fold the breast to enclose the stuffing and secure with toothpicks.

Brown the chicken in margarine over medium heat to a rich brown color on all sides. Add the stock and vinegar to the pan, cover and cook slowly for 20 minutes.

Blend the cornstarch with ½ cup of the pineapple liquid and salt, stir into the pan with the chicken and cook uncovered for 15 minutes. Add the cherries. Heat the brandy over hot water, pour over the chicken and flame before serving.

Oven Barbecued Chicken

Serves 6

⅓ cup water
⅓ cup vinegar
3 tablespoons polyunsaturated oil
½ cup chili sauce
3 tablespoons Worcestershire sauce
1 teaspoon dry mustard
½ teaspoon freshly ground black pepper
1½ teaspoons kosher salt
¼ teaspoon garlic powder
2 tablespoons brown sugar
1 frying chicken, skin removed and cut into serving pieces

Combine all the ingredients except for the chicken in a saucepan and simmer for 10 minutes over low heat.

Place the chicken in a baking pan, pour half the sauce over the chicken and bake uncovered at 350 degrees for 45 minutes. Baste with the remaining sauce every 10 minutes and continue baking uncovered for 45 minutes more.

~~

Oven Fried Chicken

Serves 6

6 ounces oyster crackers
1 cup liquid egg substitute
1 tablespoon Dijon mustard
1 teaspoon thyme
1 teaspoon kosher salt
½ teaspoon freshly ground black pepper
4 chicken thighs, skinned
4 chicken drumsticks, skinned

Pulse the oyster crackers in a food processor until broken up and transfer to a shallow bowl.

In another shallow bowl mix the egg substitute, mustard, thyme, salt and pepper. Coat the chicken pieces in the egg mixture and then roll in the cracker crumbs until coated.

Set the chicken on a baking rack, spray with vegetable spray and bake at 400 degrees for 35 minutes.

[156]

Apricot Chicken

Serves 6

6 boneless, skinless chicken breasts, halved
1 package dry leek soup mix
8 ounces Russian dressing
2 tablespoons white vinegar
12 ounces apricot jam
Rice

Place the chicken flat in a casserole and cover with the rest of the ingredients. Cover the casserole and bake at 350 degrees for 45 minutes. Serve over rice.

~~

Citrus Chicken

Serves 6

3 pounds boneless skinless chicken thighs cut into 2 inch chunks
6 tablespoons extra virgin olive oil
2 orange bell peppers, seeded and cut into 1 inch pieces
1 large red onion, peeled and cut into 1 inch pieces
1 pound mushroom caps
Zest of 3 limes
Juice of 3 limes
Juice of 1 orange
¼ cup fresh mint
1 teaspoon kosher salt
½ teaspoon freshly ground black pepper
1 cup Greek tzatziki
Wooden skewers

Whisk the lime juice, lime zest, orange juice, salt pepper, mint and olive oil together in a bowl.

Thread one piece of pepper, then one piece of onion, then one mushroom cap and then one piece of chicken onto 2 skewers until all the vegetables and chicken are used. Arrange the skewers in a baking dish and pour the citrus sauce over them. Cover and refrigerate overnight.

Grill the skewers over high heat for 3 to 4 minutes on a side until the chicken is cooked and the vegetables begin to char. Coat the skewers with tzatziki before serving.

FRAYDA FAIGEL AND HARRIS FAIGEL

Chicken Casserole

Serves 4

1 medium yellow onion, chopped
1 tablespoon polyunsaturated margarine
1 4-ounce can sliced mushrooms, drained
2 cooked chicken breasts, broken into pieces
2 ounces pimiento, sliced
¾ cup shredded Sapsago cheese
⅔ cup skim milk
½ cup corn flakes

Sauté the onion in the margarine. Combine the onion and the ingredients except for the milk and 2 tablespoons of shredded cheese and toss lightly.

Turn the mixture into a casserole, pour the milk over the casserole and sprinkle with the remaining cheese. Cover with corn flakes and bake at 375 degrees for 30 minutes.

~~

Drunken Chicken

Serves 6

1 3½ to 4 pound chicken
1 teaspoon kosher salt
½ teaspoon freshly ground black pepper
1 teaspoon garlic powder
1 teaspoon sweet paprika
⅓ teaspoon chopped dried rosemary
2 tablespoons extra virgin olive oil
1 can of beer
2 bay leaves
½ teaspoon fresh parsley
1 large Vidalia onion
6 cloves garlic
1 cup low sodium canned chicken stock

Preheat the oven to 425 degrees.
Pat the chicken dry outside and inside the cavity. Combine the salt, pepper, garlic powder and paprika. Rub 1 teaspoonful inside the cavity. Rub the outside of the chicken with the olive oil and then with the rest of the seasonings.

Place an opened can of beer upright in a roasting pan. Place the chicken over the can of beer with the can inside the cavity and the legs providing a tripod for support. Add the bay leaves, onion, garlic and ½ cup of the chicken stock to the pan and transfer the pan to the oven. After 30 minutes, add the remaining chicken stock and baste the chicken. Continue roasting for 30 to 40 minutes more until an instant meat thermometer reads 160 degrees when inserted into the thigh.

Remove the pan from the oven, tent with aluminum foil and let rest for 10 minutes. Using oven mitts, carefully remove the chicken from the very hot beer can and place on a carving board. Return the pan to the stove, skim any visible fat, add a slurry of 1 teaspoon of cornstarch mixed with 2 teaspoons of cold water, bring to boil for 5 minutes to thicken the sauce.

~~

Chicken Almandine

Serves 6

1 3-pound frying chicken, skin removed and quartered
⅔ cup polyunsaturated oil
½ cup dry sherry
1 tablespoon chopped shallots
1 cup blanched slivered almonds
1 tablespoon tomato paste
3 tablespoons flour
3 cups chicken stock
½ cup dry white wine

Brown the chicken in the oil and remove from the pan. Toast the almonds in a dry pan until lightly browned and set aside. Add the sherry, shallots and almonds to the pan which held the chicken and simmer for 10 minutes. Remove from the heat and slowly stir in the tomato paste and flour. Add the chicken stock and wine, stir thoroughly, add the chicken, cover and simmer for 40 minutes.

Poached Chicken With Quinoa

Serves 6

2 cups quinoa or farro
3 cups water
½ teaspoon kosher salt
¼ teaspoon freshly ground black pepper
½ bunch scallions, sliced
5 cups low-sodium chicken stock
Zest of 3 lemons
Juice of 3 lemons
3 cloves garlic, minced
1 tablespoon Dijon mustard
6 boneless skinless chicken breast halves
¼ cup olive oil

In a large Dutch oven, combine the quinoa, water and salt, bring to a boil, cover and simmer over low heat for 25 minutes until all the water is absorbed. Transfer the quinoa to a bowl and stir the black pepper and scallions into it.

In a large skillet, combine the chicken stock, zest and juice of one lemon and the garlic, bring to a boil, lower the heat, add the chicken and simmer for 20 minutes until an instant thermometer in the thickest part of the breast reads 165 degrees. Cut the chicken into ¾ inch slices and place on a platter.

In a bowl, whisk the mustard and remaining zest and juice and the olive oil. Stir ½ of this mixture into the quinoa and drizzle the rest over the chicken.

~~

Chicken a la Roma

Serves 6

1 4-pound chicken, skin removed and cut into 12 pieces
1 teaspoon kosher salt
½ teaspoon freshly ground white pepper
¼ cup extra virgin olive oil
1 medium yellow onion, diced
1 large carrot, cut into ¼ inch pieces
2 celery ribs, cut into ½ inch pieces
8 artichoke hearts, halved

8 garlic cloves
¼ cup sugar
1 cup red wine
½ cup wine vinegar
½ cup orange juice
1 teaspoon lemon zest
2 tablespoons capers
¼ cup pine nuts
1 tablespoon chopped fresh parsley

Season the chicken inside and out with the salt and pepper. Cook the chicken in a large deep skillet with 2 tablespoons of olive oil over medium heat until browned on all sides and remove to a platter. Add the remaining olive oil to the skillet and sauté the onion, carrot, celery, artichokes and garlic over medium heat for 8 to 10 minutes. Add the sugar, wine vinegar, orange juice, lemon zest, capers and pine nuts and bring to a boil. Return the chicken to the skillet, partially cover and simmer for 40 minutes until the chicken is cooked. Remove the chicken to a platter, skim off visible fat and boil the sauce for 3 minutes until thickened. Spoon the sauce over the chicken and garnish with parsley.

~~

Chicken Salad

Serves 4

8 ounces left-over roasted chicken, boned and diced
2 celery ribs, diced
½ medium red onion, diced
¼ sweet red pepper, cored and finely diced
1 tablespoon cucumber relish
2 tablespoons mayonnaise
½ teaspoon smoked paprika
Lettuce leaves

In a bowl, combine the chicken, celery, onion, red pepper, pickle relish and mayonnaise. Serve on lettuce leaves garnished with smoked paprika.

Chicken In Wine Sauce

Serves 6

1 3-pound broiling chicken, skin removed and cut into serving portions
1 tablespoon polyunsaturated oil
1 tablespoon extra virgin olive oil
½ cup dry vermouth
1 medium yellow onion, diced
1 teaspoon extra virgin olive oil
1 garlic clove, minced
1 tomato, chopped
½ cup dry white wine
½ cup water
½ teaspoon kosher salt
¼ teaspoon freshly ground black pepper

Sauté the chicken in the polyunsaturated oil and the olive oil until browned and drain. Pour the vermouth over the chicken and flame it. Simmer the chicken until thoroughly browned.

In a separate pan, sauté the onion in the olive oil until translucent (do not brown). Add the garlic, chopped tomato, wine and water and simmer for 10 minutes. Add the chicken, salt and pepper, cover and simmer for 30 minutes.

~~

Turkey Chili

Serves 8

¼ cup polyunsaturated oil
2 pounds ground turkey
1 medium yellow onion, diced
3 garlic cloves, minced
1 tablespoon chili powder
1 teaspoon dried oregano
¾ teaspoon chipotle powder
¼ teaspoon dried red pepper flakes
1 28-ounce can tomato puree
3 15-ounce cans pinto beans, drained
1 cup lager beer
½ cup low salt chicken stock
1 tablespoon wine vinegar
1 teaspoon dried thyme
1 teaspoon sugar

1 teaspoon kosher salt
1 teaspoon freshly ground black pepper
¼ cup shredded cheddar cheese

In a large Dutch oven, heat 1 teaspoon of the oil until shimmering and add ½ the ground turkey. Cook stirring until the meat is browned and no pink remains. Place the cooked turkey in a bowl, add 1 tablespoon of oil to the Dutch oven and brown the remaining ground turkey and add to the turkey in the bowl.

Add the remaining olive oil to the pot and sauté the onion and garlic until translucent, about 3 minutes. Add the chili powder, oregano, chipotle powder and red pepper flakes and cook for 2 minutes. Add the cooked turkey, tomato puree, beans, beer and chicken stock and bring to a boil. Stir in the broth and the vinegar, cover, reduce the heat and simmer for 45 minutes. Add the thyme, salt and pepper. Garnish each serving with 1 tablespoon of shredded cheddar cheese.

~~

Chicken La Scala

Serves 6

3 whole chicken breasts, skinned, boned and halved
2 tablespoons all-purpose flour
¼ cup polyunsaturated oil
10 ounces low salt beef stock
½ cup Greek yogurt
1 teaspoon kosher salt
¼ teaspoon freshly ground black pepper
1 tablespoon grated pecorino Romano cheese

Wipe the chicken with a dry paper towel and dredge in the flour to coat evenly. In a large skillet or Dutch oven sauté the chicken in the oil until it is golden brown on each side. Add the beef stock and simmer covered for 45 minutes. Stir in the yogurt, salt and pepper and heat thoroughly. Remove the chicken breasts to a casserole and tent with aluminum foil to keep warm. Simmer the sauce until reduced to ⅔ the original volume and pour over the chicken. Sprinkle the chicken with cheese and broil until cheese is melted and browned.

Chicken Budapest

Serves 6

1 3-pound frying chicken, skinned and cut into individual portions
¼ teaspoon freshly ground black pepper
1 teaspoon kosher salt
1½ teaspoons paprika
2 tablespoons polyunsaturated oil
1 garlic clove minced
2 tablespoons all-purpose flour
1 tablespoon polyunsaturated margarine
1½ cup chicken stock
2 tablespoons dry white wine

Season the chicken with the pepper, salt and paprika. In a skillet, sear the chicken in the oil until browned on all sides. Drain and add the garlic.

Blend the flour and margarine with the chicken stock and heat over low heat until the mixture thickens. Pour over the chicken, cover and simmer for 45 minutes. Remove the chicken, add the white wine to the skillet and bring to a boil. Pour the sauce over chicken and serve.

~~

Mushroom-Stuffed Chicken Tenders Madeira

Serves 4

2 teaspoons polyunsaturated oil
2 cups diced brown mushrooms
1 large garlic clove, minced
¼ teaspoon freshly ground black pepper
8 chicken tenders
4 ⅛-inch thick slices Gouda cheese
¾ cup low salt chicken stock
¼ cup Madeira
1 teaspoon water
1 teaspoon cornstarch
3 tablespoon scallions, chopped

Heat 1 teaspoon olive oil in a nonstick skillet over medium heat. Add the mushrooms and garlic and sauté for 2 minutes, add the pepper and set aside.

[164]

Cut a slit in each of the chicken tenders and stuff the pocket with diced mushrooms and a slice of cheese. Heat 1 teaspoon olive oil in a nonstick skillet over high heat. Add the chicken, cooking for 6 minutes on each side and set aside. Add the chicken stock and Madeira to the skillet, bring to a boil and cook until reduced to ½ cup. Combine the water and cornstarch, add to the skillet and bring to a boil. Return the chicken to the skillet, cover and simmer for 2 minutes to reheat. Garnish with scallions.

~~

Brunswick Stew

Serves 6

1 3-pound frying chicken, skinless and cut into individual portions
1½ cups chopped onion
2 garlic cloves, crushed
1 tablespoon kosher salt
¼ teaspoon freshly ground black pepper
¼ teaspoon crushed red pepper
2 cups water
3 cups potatoes, diced
1 16-ounce can diced tomatoes
1 10-ounce package frozen baby lima beans
1 10-ounce package frozen okra
1 6-ounce can tomato paste
1 12-ounce can whole kernel corn
2 tablespoons all-purpose flour
2 tablespoons polyunsaturated oil

Combine the chicken, garlic, salt, pepper, red pepper and water in a Dutch oven. Cover and simmer for 45 minutes. Remove the chicken from the broth and chill the liquid in the refrigerator until the fat hardens and can be removed. Bone the chicken and refrigerate.

Discard the fat from the broth. Add the potatoes, tomatoes, lima beans, okra, tomato paste to the broth and bring to a boil. Reduce the heat and simmer for 30 minutes. Add the corn and chicken. Blend the flour with the oil and add to the stew. Cook over medium heat stirring until thickened.

Chicken Cacciatore

Serves 4

4 chicken legs including thigh and leg, skinned and cut into separate servings
3 tablespoons polyunsaturated oil
1 clove garlic, minced
1 large onion, chopped
1 16-ounce can diced tomatoes
⅛ teaspoon thyme
¼ teaspoon marjoram
1 teaspoon oregano
1 teaspoon basil
1 bay leaf
½ cup dry white wine
½ teaspoon kosher salt
¼ teaspoon freshly ground black pepper
1 teaspoon sugar

Sauté the chicken in the oil until browned on all sides. Add the garlic and onion and cook until the onion is browned. Add the tomatoes, thyme, marjoram, oregano, basil, wine, salt, pepper and sugar. Simmer covered for 45 minutes.

~~

Duck With Blueberry Sauce

Serves 4

¼ cup granulated sugar
2 tablespoons water
2 tablespoons raspberry vinegar
1 cup low salt chicken stock
½ cup dry white wine
1 cup mixed dried fruit, cut into matchsticks
2 12-ounce boneless duck breasts
½ teaspoon kosher salt
4 teaspoons crushed red peppercorns
2 tablespoons polyunsaturated margarine
¾ cup frozen blueberries, thawed
2 tablespoons Cognac (optional)

Stir the sugar and water in a saucepan over low heat until the sugar dissolves. Increase the heat and boil until the sugar begins to turn light brown. Stir in the vinegar and mix well.

Add the stock and white wine and simmer for 20 minutes or until the sauce is reduced in half. Remove from the heat and stir in the sliced fruit. Whisk in the margarine and then stir in the blueberries and Cognac.

Pierce the skin on the duck breasts all over. Rub the peppercorns over the skin of the duck and sprinkle with salt. Cook the duck breasts in a heavy skillet, skin side down for 15 minutes until the skin is crisp. Turn the breasts over, cook for 8 minutes more, remove from the skillet and let rest.

Remove the skin and slice the duck breasts. Serve coated with the sauce.

~~

Grilled Chicken Tenders Athena

Serves 4

¼ cup polyunsaturated oil
1 pound chicken tenders
½ Vidalia onion, cut in wedges
1 teaspoon kosher salt
½ teaspoon freshly ground black pepper
Zest of 1 orange
½ teaspoon dried sage
8 Kalamata olives, pitted and chopped
½ cup dry white wine
½ cup low salt chicken stock
2 ounces feta cheese, crumbled

Heat the oil in a sauté pan over medium high heat. Add the chicken in a single layer and add the onions, salt and pepper. Sear the chicken for 30 seconds per side and reduce the heat to low. Add the orange zest and cook the chicken for 8 minutes, turning when half done.

Pour off all the fat from the pan, set over medium high heat and add the wine to deglaze the pan. When the wine has cooked off, add the stock and simmer for 15 minutes.

Spoon the sauce over the chicken for serving and sprinkle with feta cheese.

Chicken Livers Caruso

Serves 4

2 medium onions, chopped
½ pound brown mushrooms, sliced
1 medium green pepper, diced
2 cloves garlic, crushed
3 tablespoons polyunsaturated oil
1 teaspoon salt
1 tablespoon oregano
1 tablespoon julienned fresh sweet basil
½ pound chicken livers, quartered
1 28-ounce can crushed peeled tomatoes
1 tablespoon sugar
1 pound linguini
1 cup grated Romano cheese

In a heavy skillet, sauté the onions, mushrooms, green pepper and garlic in oil. Add the salt, oregano and chicken livers and cook until the livers are brown. Add the basil, tomatoes and sugar, cover and simmer for 30 minutes.

Cook the linguini in boiling salted water for 8 minutes and drain in a colander. Do not rinse. Place the linguini in a large bowl, mix in the sauce. Serve with Romano cheese.

~~

Turkey Ragu

Serves 6

1 onion, diced
2 carrots, diced
2 celery ribs, diced
1 red bell pepper, diced
4 garlic cloves, minced
2 teaspoons extra virgin olive oil
1 pound lean ground turkey
1 teaspoon dried rosemary, crumbled
½ teaspoon dried oregano, crumbled
½ cup red wine
2 14-ounce cans crushed tomatoes
2 tablespoons tomato paste
2 cups low salt beef stock
1 teaspoon kosher salt
1 tablespoon sugar

In a large skillet over medium heat, sauté the onion, carrots, celery, bell pepper and garlic in olive oil until softened and set aside. In the same pan sauté the ground turkey over medium heat until browned. Pour off any remaining fat. Add the wine and cook until most of the wine evaporates. Stir in the crushed tomatoes, tomato paste, salt, sugar and the beef stock and simmer for 15 minutes.

~~

Turkey Scaloppini

Serves 4

1 pound thin skinless turkey cutlets
2 tablespoons polyunsaturated margarine
1 pound fresh mushrooms, sliced
1 cup low salt chicken stock
½ cup chopped onion
1 large garlic clove, minced
1 tablespoon chopped flat leaf parsley
1½ teaspoons oregano
1 teaspoon salt
¼ teaspoon freshly ground black pepper
2 tablespoons all-purpose flour
⅓ cup dry white wine

One at a time, place the turkey cutlets between 2 layers of plastic wrap and pound flat, moving from the center to the edges.

In a large skillet, brown the cutlets and the mushrooms in the margarine. Add the chicken stock, onions, garlic, parsley, oregano and salt and pepper. Cook over low heat for 20 minutes until the turkey is tender. Remove the cutlets to a warm plate and cover with aluminum foil. Blend the flour and 2 tablespoons of wine and stir into the liquid in the skillet and cook until the sauce thickens. Add the rest of the wine, cook for 5 more minutes and pour over the cutlets.

Chicken Florentine

Serves 6

½ cup polyunsaturated oil
2 tablespoons lemon juice
1½ teaspoons kosher salt
½ teaspoon freshly ground black pepper
2 tablespoons minced parsley
2 pounds boneless, skinless chicken breasts
½ cup all-purpose flour
½ cup liquid egg substitute
1 10-ounce package frozen spinach

Mix 4 tablespoons oil with the lemon juice, salt, pepper and parsley in a plastic resealable bag. Add the chicken, shake well to coat the chicken and marinate in the refrigerator for 4 hours or overnight.

Dredge the chicken in the flour and then the egg substitute and brown thoroughly on all sides in a skillet in the remaining oil. Cover loosely and cook over medium heat for 15 minutes. Squeeze all the water from the spinach, chop lightly and add to the chicken.

~~

Stuffed Cornish Hens

Serves 4

¼ cup low salt chicken stock
¼ cup dry white wine
¼ teaspoon thyme
½ teaspoon chopped flat leaf parsley
2 4-ounce cans mushroom stems and pieces, drained
1 cup celery, finely chopped
1 cup freshly chopped onion
⅛ teaspoon freshly ground black pepper
½ teaspoon kosher salt
1 cup bread crumbs
½ teaspoon kosher salt
4 Rock Cornish hens

In a small bowl, combine the stock, wine, thyme, parsley and set aside.

In a large bowl, combine the mushrooms, celery, onion, pepper and salt. Add the breadcrumbs.

Remove the neck and giblets from the hens, rinse and drain well and pat dry with paper towels. Tuck the neck skin of the hens under the wings and secure them with toothpicks. Sprinkle the outside and the cavities of the hens with kosher salt. Spoon the mushroom mixture into the cavities. Tie the legs to the tail of each hen with string.

Place the hens in a roasting pan, breast side up. Pour the chicken stock over the hens and roast at 350 degrees for 1 hour, basting with the pan juices every 15 minutes. Skim the fat from the pan and serve the remaining gravy with the hens.

~~

Spiced Turkey Loaf

Serves 6

1 tablespoon polyunsaturated margarine
2 medium onions, chopped
1 pound sliced mushrooms
3 garlic cloves, diced
1 cup panko breadcrumbs
¼ cup low sodium chicken stock
1 tablespoon low-sodium soy sauce
1 tablespoon Chinese hot chili sauce
1 tablespoon Worcestershire sauce
1½ pounds ground turkey breast
1 cup liquid egg substitute
½ cup chili sauce
1 tablespoon light brown sugar
1 tablespoon Dijon mustard

Melt the margarine in a large skillet over medium heat. Add the onions, mushrooms and garlic. Cook for 6 to 8 minutes and cool. Combine this mixture with the panko, chicken stock, soy sauce, hot chili sauce, Worcestershire sauce, ground turkey and egg substitute in a large bowl. Place into a loaf pan coated with cooking spray. Combine the chili sauce, brown sugar and mustard and spread evenly over the loaf. Bake at 350 degrees for 45 minutes. Let cool for 10 to 15 minutes before serving.

Herbed Chicken

Serves 6

½ cup all-purpose flour
1 teaspoon kosher salt
1 teaspoon freshly ground black pepper
1 teaspoon chopped flat leaf parsley
½ teaspoon rosemary
½ teaspoon thyme
½ teaspoon marjoram
½ teaspoon ground coriander
3 pounds of chicken thighs and legs, skinned and cut into individual servings
⅓ cup polyunsaturated oil
Lemon slices

Combine the flour, salt, pepper, parsley, rosemary, thyme, marjoram and coriander. Pat the chicken dry with a paper towel and dredge in the flour mixture.

Add the oil to a skillet over medium high heat, add the chicken and brown well on all sides until the meat is golden. Cover, reduce the heat to low and cook for 30 minutes. Uncover and cook for 10 minutes more. Garnish with lemon slices.

~~

Chicken Marengo

Serves 6

1 3-pound frying chicken, skinned and cut into individual servings
1¼ teaspoon kosher salt
¼ teaspoon freshly ground black pepper
¼ cup polyunsaturated oil
2 cups sliced onion
1 pound sliced brown mushrooms
3 garlic cloves, minced
1 16-ounce can whole tomatoes
¾ cup dry white wine
2 tablespoons all-purpose flour

Rub the chicken with salt and pepper and brown in a skillet in the oil. Remove the chicken from the pan and drain on paper towels. In the skillet, sauté the onion, mushrooms and garlic. Add the tomatoes, cover and simmer for 30 minutes. Remove to a casserole and set aside.

Blend the flour with a small amount of liquid in the skillet, then stir in the rest of the liquid until thickened. Pour the mixture over the chicken and bake covered at 350 degrees for 20 minute.

~~

Crusty Turkey Cutlets

Serves 4

1 pound thin skinless turkey cutlets
1 teaspoon kosher salt
½ teaspoon paprika
1 cup grape nuts cereal, lightly crushed
1 cup Parmesan cheese
1 tablespoon minced flat leaf parsley
½ cup liquid egg substitute
2 tablespoons polyunsaturated oil
Lemon wedges

Combine the paprika and salt and rub into the cutlets. One at a time, place the cutlets between clear plastic wrap and pound flat, beginning in the center and moving to the edges.

Combine the crushed grape nuts, Parmesan cheese and parsley. Dry the cutlets, dip in the egg substitute and then dredge in the crumb mixture.

Sauté the cutlets in hot oil for 3-4 minutes on each side. Drain on paper towels and serve garnished with lemon wedges.

FRAYDA FAIGEL AND HARRIS FAIGEL

Honey Glazed Chicken

Serves 6

1 3-pound frying chicken, skinned and cut into individual servings
1 cup honey
¼ cup Dijon mustard
¼ cup lemon juice

Mix the honey, mustard and lemon juice together and coat the chicken with half. Bake the chicken at 350 degrees for one hour, basting every 10 minutes with the honey mixture.

Chapter XIV - Vegetables

Artichokes In Orange Sauce

Serves 4

4 medium artichokes
1½ cups low salt chicken stock
⅓ cup orange juice
1 tablespoon cornstarch
½ teaspoon kosher salt

Clean and trim the artichokes and place in one inch of water in a large saucepan, stems down. Cover and simmer for 30 minutes.

Combine the chicken stock, orange juice, cornstarch and salt. Cook over medium heat until the mixture begins to boil and is thickened.

Halve the steamed artichokes, remove the choke and pour the sauce over the artichokes.

~~

Lemon Spinach

Serves 4

1 pound fresh or frozen spinach, washed and drained
Zest of one lemon
Juice of one lemon
2 teaspoons extra virgin olive oil
½ teaspoon kosher salt

In a large covered pot with a colander, steam the spinach for 3 to 5 minutes until it begins to wilt. Place the spinach in a bowl and mix in the olive oil and then the lemon zest, lemon juice and salt.

Steamed Brussels Sprouts

Serves 6

1 pound Brussels sprouts
1 tablespoon polyunsaturated oil
½ teaspoon kosher salt
2 tablespoons freshly squeezed lemon or lime juice

Wash the Brussels sprouts, cut in half through the stem and drain, but do not dry. Place the sprouts in a bowl, cover with plastic wrap and microwave at full power for 10 minutes. Uncover and drain the water from the bowl. Add the oil, salt and lemon or lime juice, mix well and serve.

~~

Eggplant Parmigiana

Serves 6

1 large eggplant, peeled and cut into ½ inch slices
2 tablespoons polyunsaturated oil
1 cup Italian seasoned breadcrumbs
½ teaspoon garlic powder
½ teaspoon kosher salt
¼ teaspoon freshly ground black pepper
¼ cup grated Parmesan cheese
½ cup part-skim mozzarella cheese
Tomato sauce
1 16-ounce can crushed tomatoes
1 small can tomato paste
1 teaspoon dried oregano
1 teaspoon dried basil
¼ teaspoon salt
1 teaspoon sugar

Brush the eggplant with oil and broil until lightly browned.

sauce: place the tomatoes, tomato paste, oregano, basil, salt and sugar in a sauce pan and bring to a boil. Lower the heat and simmer for 10 minutes. Mix the breadcrumbs, garlic powder, salt, pepper and Parmesan cheese together.

Place a layer of one half of the eggplant on the bottom of a casserole and spread a layer of tomato sauce. Sprinkle with half the breadcrumb mixture and then with a layer of mozzarella. Place a layer of the remaining eggplant on top of the cheese, spread with tomato sauce, sprinkle with the remaining breadcrumb mixture and top with the mozzarella. Bake for 25 minutes at 375 degrees and let cool for 10 minutes before slicing.

~~

Glazed Sweet Potatoes

Serves 6

 6 canned sweet potatoes, sliced
 1 orange, peeled and sliced
 1 cup orange juice
 2 teaspoons grated orange rind
 ⅓ cup brown sugar
 1 tablespoon cornstarch
 ⅓ cup granulated sugar
 ¼ teaspoon kosher salt

Place the sweet potatoes and orange slices in a glass baking dish.

Mix the orange juice, orange rind and salt. Add the brown sugar, cornstarch and granulated sugar and pour this sauce over the sweet potatoes and oranges. Bake covered for one hour at 350 degrees, uncover and bake for 30 minutes more.

~~

Roasted Beets

Serves 6

 6 large beets
 1 tablespoon polyunsaturated oil

Wash the beets thoroughly and dry them. Rub each beet with the oil and wrap them separately in aluminum foil. Roast for one hour at 350 degrees and cool.

When the beets are cool enough to handle, open the foil and rub each one with a paper towel to remove the skin. Slice the beets and serve warm or cut into ½ inch cubes to add to salads.

Balsamic Beets

Serves 6

6 beets
3 tablespoons extra virgin olive oil
½ teaspoon fresh rosemary
½ teaspoon fresh thyme
3 cloves garlic, halved
½ teaspoon kosher salt
¼ teaspoon freshly ground black pepper
¼ pound goat cheese
4 teaspoons balsamic vinegar
Lettuce or endive leaves

Rub the beets with olive oil, wrap in aluminum foil with the rosemary, thyme, garlic cloves, salt and pepper and roast for one hour at 350 degrees. Allow to cool and rub the beets with a paper towel to remove the skin.

Dice the beets. Mix in the goat cheese and balsamic vinegar and serve on lettuce or endive leaves.

~~

Scalloped Potatoes

Serves 6

2 large potatoes, peeled and thinly sliced
1 tablespoon polyunsaturated oil
1½ tablespoons rice flour or 2 tablespoons all-purpose flour
¼ teaspoon kosher salt
½ cup concentrated soy protein infant formula
½ cup water
2 tablespoons low fat Asiago cheese

Blend the oil, flour and salt and cook over a low heat, slowly blending in the infant formula and water to avoid lumps. Cook until the sauce is smooth and thickened.

Place ⅓ of the potatoes in a casserole and pour ⅓ of the sauce over them. Add a second layer of potatoes and another ⅓ of the sauce. Finish with a third layer of potatoes and the rest of the sauce. Sprinkle the cheese and bake covered at 350 degrees for one hour. Uncover the potatoes and continue baking until the potatoes are browned.

Potato Pancakes

Serves 6

5 large potatoes, peeled, grated and drained, liquid reserved
½ cup liquid egg substitute
1 teaspoon kosher salt
1 tablespoon all-purpose flour
1 tablespoon minced onion
½ teaspoon baking powder
2 tablespoons polyunsaturated oil
Applesauce

Mix the drained potatoes, egg substitute, salt, flour, onion and baking powder. If the consistency is too thick, add some of the reserved potato liquid.

Drop the mixture by the tablespoonful into the oil in a hot skillet and brown well on both sides. Drain on a paper towel to remove excess oil. Serve with applesauce.

~~

Home Fried Potatoes

Serves 6

2 medium baking potatoes
2 tablespoons polyunsaturated oil
1 medium white onion, diced
½ teaspoon paprika
1 teaspoon kosher salt
2 tablespoons chopped chives

Pierce the potatoes several times with a fork and microwave at high heat for 4 minutes. Cool and dice into ¼ inch pieces.

In a bowl, mix the potatoes and oil until all the pieces are coated. Sauté the potatoes in a skillet over medium high heat until browned, about 10 minutes. Stir in the onions, reduce the heat to medium and sauté until the onions are translucent, about 10 minutes. Stir in the paprika and salt. Garnish with chives. Serve hot.

Parsnip And Potato Puree

Serves 6

1 pound parsnips, peeled and sliced
1 pound white potatoes, peeled and diced
1 teaspoon kosher salt
½ teaspoon white pepper
1 cup nonfat milk
½ cup low fat sour cream
4 cloves garlic, peeled and smashed
1 bay leaf
½ teaspoon dry thyme
¼ pound stick of polyunsaturated margarine
2 tablespoons extra virgin olive oil
Parsley

Place the parsnips and potatoes in a casserole, add the salt, pepper, milk, garlic, bay leaf and thyme and simmer over medium heat for 15 minutes.

Place the cooked parsnips, potatoes and margarine in a food processor. Remove the bay leaf and add ½ cup of the milk mixture to the processor. Add the sour cream and puree the parsnips and potatoes. Add more milk mixture until the puree reaches the texture of whipped cream. Pour into a serving bowl and garnish with parsley.

~~

Baked Beans

Serves 6

2 pounds pea beans
Water to cover
2 tablespoons polyunsaturated oil
1 medium onion
8 tablespoons granulated sugar
⅔ cup molasses
2 tablespoons dry mustard
4 teaspoons kosher salt
½ teaspoon freshly ground black pepper

Soak the beans overnight in water. In the morning, parboil the beans in the water for 10 minutes and strain. Reserve the water.

Put the oil and onion in a bean pot and add the beans. Mix the remaining ingredients with 1 cup of reserved water, pour over the beans and bake for six hours at 300 degrees. Continue to add water as needed to keep the beans from drying out.

~~

Arugula And Tangerine Salad

Serves 4

½ cup walnut halves
¼ cup cashews halved
1 large bunch arugula, coarsely chopped
2 large tangerines, peeled, seeded and sectioned
8 fresh figs, quartered
½ cup sliced red onion
½ cup extra virgin olive oil
⅔ cup orange juice
¼ cup sugar
2 tablespoons balsamic vinegar
2 teaspoons Dijon mustard
¼ teaspoon dried oregano
¼ teaspoon freshly ground white pepper
⅓ cup crumbled cambozola blue cheese

Toast the nuts in a nonstick skillet for 5 minutes until lightly browned. Toss the toasted nuts, arugala, tangerine sections, figs and red onion in a large bowl.

Mix the olive oil, orange juice, sugar, balsamic vinegar, mustard, oregano and pepper in a covered jar and shake well until thoroughly mixed. Drizzle with the dressing and sprinkle each serving with the blue cheese.

Bulgur Pilaf

Serves 6

1 cup cracked bulgur wheat
¼ cup polyunsaturated margarine
1 teaspoon kosher salt
¼ teaspoon freshly ground black pepper
2½ cups low salt chicken stock
1 6-ounce can tomato paste
Low-fat Greek yogurt

Melt the margarine in a large saucepan and sauté the bulgur wheat with the salt and pepper until lightly browned. Add the tomato paste and chicken stock and bring to a boil. Cover and reduce the heat. Simmer for 30 minutes until the wheat is tender and all the liquid is absorbed. Let stand for 15 minutes before serving.
Serve with the yogurt.

~~

Popcorn Cauliflower

Serves 4

1 large cauliflower
3 tablespoons extra virgin olive oil
1 teaspoon kosher salt
¼ teaspoon freshly ground white pepper
6 drops Tabasco sauce

Trim all the flowerets around the cauliflower into popcorn sized bites. Mix the cauliflower, oil, salt, pepper and Tabasco in a bowl to thoroughly coat the flowerets. Spread the cauliflower on a sheet pan and roast at 450 degrees for 1 hour, turning every 15 minutes until the cauliflower is browned and crisp. Serve hot.

Broccoli Casserole

Serves 6

5 10-ounce packages frozen broccoli
½ cup skim milk
1 10-ounce can cream of mushroom soup undiluted
1 cup unflavored breadcrumbs
½ cup liquid egg substitute, cooked in a pan and chopped
⅛ pound polyunsaturated margarine, melted

Cut the broccoli into serving-size pieces. Place the broccoli in the bottom of a glass baking dish and add the milk and mushroom soup. Cover the broccoli with the chopped egg, top with breadcrumbs and melted margarine. Bake for 1 hour at 350 degrees.

~~

Ratatouille Niçoise

Serves 6

¼ cup polyunsaturated oil
3 garlic cloves
3 large onions cut into rings
3 green peppers
1 medium eggplant, peeled and sliced into ½ inch cubes
2 medium zucchini, cut into ½ inch cubes
1 yellow summer squash, cut into ½ inch cubes
1 16-ounce can diced tomatoes
1 6-ounce can tomato paste
1 tablespoon basil
½ teaspoon kosher salt
¼ teaspoon freshly ground black pepper

In a Dutch oven, sauté the garlic cloves in 3 tablespoons of oil until they are translucent. Add one layer at a time of each of the vegetables, tomato paste and the diced tomatoes, sprinkling each layer with basil, salt and pepper. Add the remaining oil over the top, cover and cook over low heat for 30 minutes. Stir occasionally to prevent sticking. Serve hot or chilled.

Rice Cancun

Serves 6

1¼ cups uncooked rice
3 tablespoons polyunsaturated margarine
½ cup chopped onion
¼ cup diced green pepper
2 garlic cloves, crushed
2½ cups hot water
1 16-ounce can crushed tomatoes
1½ teaspoons kosher salt
2 teaspoons chili powder

Melt the margarine in a large saucepan. Add the rice, onion, garlic and green pepper. Cook stirring over low heat until the rice browns. Add the hot water, tomatoes, salt and chili powder, bring to a boil, cover and reduce the heat, cooking until the rice is tender and the liquid is absorbed, about 35 minutes.

~~

Chick Peas, Chard And Tomatoes

Serves 6

2 tablespoons extra virgin olive oil
2 shallots, chopped
3 scallions, chopped
½ cup chickpeas, drained
1 teaspoon kosher salt
½ teaspoon freshly ground white pepper
1 bunch chard, rinsed and coarsely chopped
1 large beefsteak tomato, sliced
Juice and zest of ½ lemon
3 tablespoons freshly grated Parmesan cheese

Heat the olive oil in a large skillet, stir in the shallots and scallions and sauté until the shallots are translucent. Add the chickpeas, salt and pepper and heat until warm. Add the chard and cook over medium heat until it is wilted. Add the tomato slices, juice and zest of the lemon and stir well. Garnish with Parmesan cheese.

Creamed Turnips

Serves 6

1 pound turnips, cleaned and peeled
1 cup water
1 teaspoon kosher salt
2 tablespoons all-purpose flour
½ cup skim milk
⅛ teaspoon freshly ground black pepper
1 teaspoon grated orange peel
½ cup chopped flat leaf parsley

Slice the turnips into ⅛-inch slices and heat in a large saucepan, with the water and ½ teaspoon of salt over high heat until boiling. Reduce the heat, cover and cook for 10 minutes until the turnips are fork tender.

Drain the turnips, reserving ½ cup of the liquid.

In a medium saucepan, stir the skim milk and flour until well-mixed. Add the reserved liquid and cook over medium heat, stirring constantly until thickened. Stir in the orange peel and turnips and pour into a serving dish. Sprinkle with the parsley.

~~

Maple Lemon Carrots

Serves 6

3 cups thinly sliced carrots into coins
½ cup water
1 tablespoon sugar
½ teaspoon kosher salt
2 tablespoons polyunsaturated margarine
2 tablespoon pure maple syrup
2 tablespoons freshly squeezed lemon juice
¼ teaspoon grated lemon peel

Combine the carrots, water, sugar and salt in a heavy saucepan. Cover and cook over medium heat until the water evaporates. Add the margarine, maple syrup, lemon juice and lemon peel, heat and stir until the margarine is melted.

Spinach Pie

Serves 6

1 10-ounce package frozen spinach
2 carrots, grated
¼ cup liquid egg substitute
1 tablespoon polyunsaturated oil
1 medium potato, grated and drained of liquid
½ small onion
¼ teaspoon kosher salt
⅛ teaspoon freshly ground black pepper
3 cups cornflakes
2 tablespoons cold polyunsaturated margarine

Mix the spinach with all the ingredients except for the cornflakes and margarine.

Place the cornflakes in a plastic baggy and crush. Pour the crushed flakes into a bowl and blend in the cold margarine. Coat the bottom of a 9-inch pie pan with the cornflakes and bake for 10 minutes at 350 degrees and cool. Fill the pie with the spinach mixture, sprinkle with additional cornflakes and bake for 30 minutes at 375 degrees.

~~

Baked "French Fries"

Serves 6

1½ pounds potatoes, peeled
2 tablespoons polyunsaturated oil
½ teaspoon kosher salt
¼ teaspoon smoky paprika

Cut the potatoes into thick strips, cover with water in a bowl and refrigerate for one hour.

Drain the potatoes and pat dry with a paper towel. Place the drained potatoes and oil in a large plastic bag, seal it and shake well until the potatoes are coated with oil.

Distribute the potatoes evenly on a cookie sheet. Bake for 40 minutes at 450 degrees, turning the potatoes several times. Sprinkle with salt and paprika before serving.

Green Beans With Pimiento And Black Olives

Serves 6

1 package of frozen French green beans
1 tablespoon polyunsaturated margarine
½ cup sliced onions
½ teaspoon kosher salt
1 small can sliced black olives
½ teaspoon capers
1 pimiento cut in strips

Melt the margarine in a saucepan. Add the onions and sauté until lightly browned. Add the green beans and salt, cover and cook until tender. Stir in the black olives, capers and pimiento and cook over low heat for 2-3 minutes until warm.

~~

Baked Stuffed Potatoes

Serves 6

6 large Idaho potatoes
¾ cup liquid egg substitute
4 tablespoons skim milk
¾ cup polyunsaturated margarine
½ teaspoon kosher salt
½ teaspoon freshly ground black pepper
½ teaspoon paprika
3 tablespoons grated Asiago low fat cheese

Spear the potatoes with a fork, microwave the potatoes for 5 minutes at full power and let cool.

Cut the potatoes in half and scoop out the pulp into a blender. Reserve the shells. Add the egg substitute, skim milk, margarine, salt and pepper and whip until smooth. Fill the shells with the whipped potato mixture, sprinkle with paprika and cheese and bake for 30 minutes at 350 degrees until the cheese is brown.

Kidney Bean And Zucchini Salad

Serves 6

3 zucchini, sliced thinly
1 large green pepper cut into 2 inch pieces
½ red onion
3 tablespoons polyunsaturated oil
1 16-ounce can kidney beans, drained and rinsed
3 tablespoons red wine vinegar
2 teaspoons sugar
2 teaspoons kosher salt
¼ teaspoon freshly ground black pepper

Sauté the zucchini, green pepper and onion in oil for 8 minutes. Add the kidney beans, vinegar, sugar, salt and pepper. Combine and chill before serving.

~~

Baked Eggplant

Serves 4

1 large eggplant, peeled and cut into ¼ inch pieces
¼ cup liquid egg substitute
½ cup unflavored breadcrumbs
¼ teaspoon oregano
¼ teaspoon basil
¼ teaspoon thyme
½ teaspoon kosher salt
½ teaspoon paprika
½ teaspoon garlic powder
1 tablespoon polyunsaturated margarine

Dip the eggplant pieces in the egg substitute and then into a mixture of breadcrumbs, oregano, basil, thyme, salt, paprika and garlic powder. Place the coated eggplant in a single layer in a shallow pan greased with margarine. Bake for 20 minutes at 400 degrees until tender.

~~

Whipped Cauliflower

Serves 6

1 large cauliflower, quartered and cored
½ cup nonfat milk
2 tablespoon extra virgin olive oil
1 teaspoon kosher salt
¼ cup flat leaf parsley, chopped

Cut the cauliflower in chunks and roast in a 350 degree oven for 45 minutes.

Cool the cauliflower and puree in a food processor. Add the milk, olive oil and salt and pulse the processor to mix thoroughly.

Garnish with parsley.

~~
Mushrooms And Peas

Serves 6

2 tablespoons polyunsaturated margarine
1 pound brown mushrooms
½ teaspoon kosher salt
2 10-ounce packages frozen peas

Melt the margarine in a saucepan. Add the sliced mushrooms and salt and sauté until mushrooms begin to brown. Add the peas and continue to heat until the peas are cooked, but still crunchy, about 15 minutes.

~~
Tomatoes Rockefeller

Serves 4

2 large ripe tomatoes, cut in half
1½ tablespoons finely chopped onion
1½ tablespoons chopped flat leaf parsley
1½ tablespoons polyunsaturated margarine
½ cup frozen spinach, drained and chopped
½ teaspoon kosher salt
¼ teaspoon freshly ground black pepper
½ teaspoon paprika
2 tablespoons panko

Place the tomatoes in a shallow baking pan, cut side up. Mix the onion, parsley, margarine, spinach, salt, pepper and paprika and spread evenly over the tomatoes. Top with the panko. Bake for 15 minutes at 375 degrees until the panko is toasted.

Kalamata Olives And Tomatoes

Serves 4

2 large tomatoes, cored and sliced thinly
½ teaspoon kosher salt
6 ounces feta cheese, crumbled
2 tablespoons extra virgin olive oil
12 Kalamata olives, pitted and halved

Arrange the tomatoes spread out on a platter. Sprinkle with salt and then spread the feta cheese over the tomatoes. Drizzle with olive oil and warm under a broiler for 2 minutes. Garnish with olives.

~~

Risotto Milanese

Serves 4

½ small onion, finely chopped
3 tablespoons polyunsaturated oil
2 cups uncooked long grain rice
Pinch saffron
2 cups chicken broth
¼ teaspoon kosher salt

Sauté the onion in the oil until golden. Add the rice and saffron and cook stirring until the rice is translucent. Cover the rice with the chicken broth, sprinkle with salt and simmer for 25 minutes, stirring occasionally, until the rice absorbs the liquid.

~~

Steamed Broccoli

Serves 6

2 pounds broccoli crowns
1 tablespoon polyunsaturated oil
½ teaspoon kosher salt
2 tablespoons freshly squeezed lemon juice

Cut the ends off the bottom ends of the broccoli spears, divide into serving-sized pieces and rinse thoroughly.

Place the broccoli in a bowl, cover with clear plastic wrap and microwave at full power for 6 minutes. Uncover and drain the water from the bowl. Add the oil, salt and lemon juice, mix well and serve.

~~

Cabbage Kiev

Serves 4

1 small green cabbage
2 tablespoons polyunsaturated oil
2 tablespoons caraway seeds
½ teaspoon kosher salt

Remove any wilted leaves from the outside of the cabbage. Cut the cabbage into quarters, remove the core and slice the cabbage triangles starting at the bottom into ¾ inch wide strips.

In a nonstick pan, heat the oil until glistening and sauté the cabbage for 25 to minutes until fork tender. Stir in the caraway seeds and salt and sauté for one minute more.

~~

Stuffed Acorn Squash

Serves 4

2 acorn squash, cut in half, seeds removed
1 cup unsweetened applesauce
4 teaspoons brown sugar
¼ cup dried plums, minced
2 teaspoons freshly squeezed lemon juice
4 teaspoons polyunsaturated margarine
Cinnamon to taste

Place the acorn squash cut side down in a shallow baking pan. Cover the bottom of the pan with water and bake for one hour at 400 degrees. Cool.

Fill the squash with applesauce, plums, brown sugar and lemon juice. Top each one with a tablespoon of margarine. Bake for 10 to 15 minutes until the applesauce is bubbly.

Sprinkle cinnamon on top before serving.

FRAYDA FAIGEL AND HARRIS FAIGEL

Pan Stuffing

Serves 6

1 8-ounce package herb-seasoned stuffing mix
¼ cup low salt chicken stock
1 medium onion
2 stalks celery, chopped
½ cup chestnut meat, chopped
½ teaspoon kosher salt
¼ teaspoon freshly ground black pepper
½ teaspoon marjoram
½ teaspoon sage
½ cup liquid egg substitute
½ cup nonfat milk
1 4-ounce cup mushrooms, drained

Cook the onion and celery in the chicken stock until softened. Add the remaining ingredients and mix well. Bake uncovered in a shallow pan at 375 degrees for 15 minutes.

Chapter XV - Salads

Beet Salad

Serves 6

1 pound fresh beets
1 small onion, chopped
¼ cup plus 1 tablespoon polyunsaturated oil
¼ cup vinegar
½ teaspoon kosher salt
2 teaspoons crumbled cambozola cheese
4 teaspoons walnuts, chopped

Oil the beets with 1 tablespoon oil, wrap in aluminum foil and roast at 350 degrees for one hour. Unwrap, cool for 10 minutes and rub with a paper towel to remove the skin of the beets.

Slice the beets and mix in a bowl with the onions. Blend the remaining oil with the vinegar and salt and pour over the beets. Refrigerate for 2 hours before serving. Garnish with the cambozola cheese and walnuts.

~~

Onion Rings Valenciana

Serves 6

3 pounds large sweet white onions
3 cups sugar
½ cup white vinegar
1 teaspoon kosher salt

Cut the onions into thin slices and separate into rings in a large bowl. Pour the sugar, vinegar and salt over the onions, mix well, cover and refrigerate for 24 hours. Chill and serve over sliced tomatoes.

Chicken Salad

Serves 6

½ cup low fat Greek yogurt
¼ cup mayonnaise
½ teaspoon kosher salt
¼ teaspoon curry powder
1 tablespoon skim milk
2½ cups cooked diced chicken
1 cup diced celery
2 tablespoons chopped red onion
½ cup slivered almonds
Belgian endive leaves

Mix together the yogurt, mayonnaise, salt, curry powder and milk. Add the chicken, celery and onion and toss well. Chill thoroughly.

Toast the almonds in a dry sauté pan over medium heat until beginning to brown.

Before serving, mix in the almonds and spoon onto the endive leaves.

~~

Marinated Cucumbers

Serves 6

3 cups sliced cucumber
1 medium green pepper, seeded and cut into rings
1 medium red onion, sliced
3 tablespoons polyunsaturated oil
2 tablespoons vinegar
2 tablespoons freshly squeezed lemon juice
1 teaspoon sugar
¼ teaspoon dill seeds
4 radishes, sliced
Iceberg lettuce leaves

In a large bowl, combine the cucumber, green pepper and onion. Blend together the oil, vinegar, lemon juice, sugar and dill, pour over the vegetables and toss. Cover and refrigerate for 1 hour. Toss before serving on lettuce leaves garnished with radish slices.

Corn Salad

Serves 4

4 ears of sweet corn, husked
¼ cup finely chopped green onions
¼ cup chopped pimientos
½ cup chopped green peppers
¼ cup diced cucumbers
¾ cup French dressing

Steam the ears of corn in a large covered pot for 15 minutes. Cool and remove the kernels from the cobs with a sharp knife.

Combine the corn with the remaining ingredients and mix well. Refrigerate for 3 hours. Drain and mix again before serving.

~~

Spinach Salad

Serves 4

1 package of fresh spinach, torn into bite-sized pieces
¾ teaspoon kosher salt
½ teaspoon sugar
⅛ teaspoon dry mustard powder
⅛ teaspoon freshly ground black pepper
1 garlic clove, crushed
3 tablespoons freshly squeezed lemon juice
1 tablespoon water
½ cup extra virgin olive oil
¼ cup chopped onion
2 cups sliced mushrooms
2 cups sliced radishes

Combine the salt, sugar, dry mustard, pepper, garlic, lemon juice, water, oil and onion in a jar. Cover and shake until thoroughly mixed and chill.

Before serving, combine the spinach, mushrooms and radishes in a large bowl. Pour the dressing over the vegetables and mix well.

Garden Salad

Serves 4

½ iceberg lettuce, halved, cored and cut into ½ inch slices
½ red lettuce cut into ½ inch slices
2 medium tomatoes cut into eighths
½ red onion halved and sliced
2 stalks celery, cut into ½ inch pieces
1 carrot, peeled and cut into ⅛ inch coins
½ sweet green pepper, seeded and cut into ¼ inch squares
½ sweet red pepper, seeded and cut into ¼ inch squares
8 mushroom caps, quartered
4 radishes, thinly sliced
3 stalks of scallions, cut into ½ inch pieces
2 tablespoons chickpeas

Mix all the ingredients in a large bowl. Serve with a vinaigrette salad dressing on the side.

~~

Cabbage Slaw

Serves 6

3 tablespoons cider vinegar
1 teaspoon sugar
1 teaspoon kosher salt
¼ teaspoon tarragon
1 head of green cabbage, shredded
1 large red apple, cut into bite sized pieces

In a covered 12-inch skillet over medium heat, warm the vinegar, sugar, salt and tarragon for 5 minutes. Add the cabbage, increase the heat and cook for 15 minutes until the cabbage is tender-crisp. Remove from the heat, stir in the apple and serve.

~~

Chickpea Salad

Serves 4

1 16-ounce can of chickpeas (garbanzo beans)
1 small red onion, finely chopped
2 teaspoons flat leaf parsley, minced

¼ cup extra virgin olive oil
3 tablespoons freshly squeezed lemon juice
¼ teaspoon kosher salt

Drain and rinse the chickpeas, place in a bowl, add the onion and parsley and mix well. Blend the oil, lemon juice and salt until creamy and pour over the chickpeas. Serve at room temperature.

~~
Cucumber Salad

Serves 4

1 cup low fat yogurt
1 teaspoon freshly squeezed lemon juice
¼ teaspoon kosher salt
3 medium cucumbers, peeled and sliced very thin
1 tablespoon chopped fresh dill weed

Blend the yogurt, lemon juice, dill and salt in a bowl and chill. Combine the cucumber with the yogurt mixture and garnish with dill.

~~
Tomato Salad

Serves 4

2 pounds tomatoes, sliced
1 large red onion, chopped
2 tablespoons freshly chopped flat parsley
1 tablespoon freshly squeezed lemon juice
3 tablespoons extra virgin olive oil
¼ teaspoon kosher salt
2 cloves garlic, crushed
½ teaspoon dried mint
1 cup toasted bread croutons

Mix the tomatoes, onion, parsley and mint in a bowl. Blend the lemon juice, oil, salt and garlic and pour over the tomatoes. Just before serving, mix in the croutons.

Marinated Mushrooms

Serves 6

⅓ cup red wine vinegar
½ cup polyunsaturated oil
1 garlic clove, minced
1 teaspoon kosher salt
½ teaspoon freshly ground black pepper
1 bay leaf
¼ teaspoon thyme
1 pound white mushrooms, sliced

Mix all the ingredients in a large bowl, cover and refrigerate for 2 hours. Discard the bay leaf. Drain and reserve the marinade to use as a salad dressing. Serve cold.

~~

Moroccan Salad

Serves 4

2 oranges, peeled, seeded and thinly sliced
1 bunch radishes, thinly sliced
1 tablespoon freshly squeezed lemon juice
¼ teaspoon kosher salt

Cut the orange slices into sections, mix with the remaining ingredients and chill.

~~

Potato Salad

Serves 6

3 cups diced potatoes
1 cup diced celery
¾ cup mayonnaise
½ cup diced sweet gherkins
1 tablespoon minced red onion
1 tablespoon white vinegar
1 teaspoon kosher salt
1 teaspoon salad style yellow mustard

Toss all the ingredients together. Chill well before serving.

Chapter XVI - Salad Dressings And Toppings

Garlic French Dressing

Serves 6

¼ teaspoon kosher salt
¼ teaspoon freshly ground black pepper
1 teaspoon Grey Poupon mustard
¼ teaspoon sugar
1 garlic clove, crushed
1 tablespoon water
3 tablespoons white vinegar
½ cup extra virgin oil

Combine all the ingredients in a jar, cover and shake well until thoroughly blended.

~~

French Dressing (2)

Serves 6

¾ cup extra virgin olive oil
¾ cup white vinegar
1 teaspoon kosher salt
1 teaspoon sugar
1 teaspoon paprika
½ teaspoon dry mustard
⅛ teaspoon cayenne pepper

Combine the vinegar, oil, salt, sugar, paprika mustard and pepper in a small jar. Cover and shake vigorously to mix well. Refrigerate. Shake well before using.

French Dressing (3)

Serves 6

3 tablespoons red wine vinegar
1 teaspoon sugar
½ teaspoon garlic powder
2 tablespoons chili sauce
1 teaspoon Worcestershire sauce
½ teaspoon kosher salt
½ cup extra virgin olive oil

Mix the first six ingredients and let stand for ½ hour. Beat in the oil until blended and chill before serving.

~~

French Dressing (4)

Serves 6

2 tablespoons cornstarch
1 tablespoon kosher salt
4 teaspoons paprika
½ teaspoon dry mustard
¼ teaspoon freshly ground black pepper
1 garlic clove, crushed
½ cup red wine vinegar
½ cup extra virgin olive oil
2 cups water

In a 1-quart saucepan, stir all the ingredients together. Cook, stirring constantly, over medium heat until slightly thickened. Cover and refrigerate. Shake well before serving. Serve within one week.

~~

Remoulade

Serves 6

3 tablespoons white vinegar
1 tablespoon Dijon mustard
1 teaspoon white horseradish
2 tablespoons scallions, minced
2 tablespoons celery, minced
1 tablespoon flat leaf parsley, minced
½ cup polyunsaturated oil

¼ teaspoon kosher salt
¼ teaspoon freshly ground black pepper
⅛ teaspoon cayenne pepper

Combine the first six ingredients in a bowl. Beat in the oil a little at a time. Add the salt, pepper and cayenne and mix well. Serve cold over seafood.

~~

Herb Dressing

Serves 6

2 teaspoons flat leaf parsley
½ teaspoon basil
½ teaspoon oregano
½ teaspoon tarragon
½ teaspoon thyme
1 tablespoon ketchup
¼ cup water
¾ cup extra virgin olive oil
¼ cup white vinegar
1 teaspoon sugar
¼ teaspoon dry mustard

Place the parsley, basil, oregano, tarragon, ketchup and thyme in a jar, add the water and let stand for 15 minutes. Add the remaining ingredients, cover and shake vigorously to blend. Refrigerate. Shake well again before using.

~~

Blender Mayonnaise

Serves 6

½ cup liquid egg substitute
¾ teaspoon kosher salt
½ teaspoon dry mustard
¼ teaspoon paprika
2 teaspoons freshly squeezed lemon juice
1 cup polyunsaturated oil

Place the egg substitute, spices, lemon juice and ¼ cup oil in a blender. Cover and run at low speed just until blended. Slowly add the remaining oil in a steady stream while the blender continues to run.

Italian Dressing

Serves 6

½ cup onion, finely chopped
2 garlic cloves, crushed
¼ cup sugar
1 cup red wine vinegar
1 cup ketchup
1 cup extra virgin olive oil
2 teaspoons kosher salt
1 teaspoon dry mustard
1 teaspoon paprika
1 teaspoon oregano

Combine all the ingredients in a jar, cover and shake well to blend. Refrigerate for 2 hours and then strain to remove the onion and garlic. Refrigerate. Shake well before using.

~~

Béchamel Sauce

Serves 6

1 cup low salt chicken stock
1 bay leaf
¾ teaspoon flat leaf parsley, minced
¼ teaspoon ground white pepper
1 carrot, peeled and sliced
2 tablespoons flour
2 tablespoons polyunsaturated margarine
½ cup evaporated milk
¼ teaspoon kosher salt
¼ teaspoon freshly ground black pepper
⅛ teaspoon garlic powder

Place the first six ingredients in a sauce pan and simmer covered for 15 minutes. Strain and set aside. Melt the margarine and add the flour until blended. Add the stock, milk, salt, pepper and garlic powder. Stir until thickened.

Chapter XVII - Noodles

Cheese Noodle Pudding

Serves 6

½ pound broad noodles, cooked
½ pound low-fat cottage cheese
½ pint low-fat yogurt
¾ cup liquid egg substitute
1 cup white raisins
2 tablespoons sugar
2 ounces polyunsaturated margarine
¼ teaspoon kosher salt

Combine all ingredients and pour into a baking dish greased with margarine. Bake for 15 minutes at 400 degrees; then reduce the heat and continue to bake for one hour at 350 degrees.

~~

Kasha Varnishkes (Groats And Noodles)

Serves 6

1 medium yellow onion, minced
1 cup polyunsaturated oil
¼ cup liquid egg substitute
2 cups water
1 teaspoon kosher salt
1 cup groats
½ cup bowtie noodles, cooked

Sauté the onions in oil. Mix the groats and egg substitute and add to the onions. Add the water and salt and bring to a boil. Cook covered over low heat for 15 minutes. Stir in the noodles.

Place the noodles in a casserole and bake for 20 minutes.

[203]

Potato Kugel (1)

Serves 8

½ cup minced onion
½ cup minced celery
3 tablespoons polyunsaturated margarine
½ teaspoon kosher salt
⅛ teaspoon freshly ground black pepper
½ teaspoon paprika
¾ cup liquid egg substitute
1 cup low-salt chicken stock
4 matzos, broken into small pieces
2 cups mashed potatoes

Sauté the onion and celery in the margarine until tender and translucent. Add the salt, pepper and paprika. Combine the egg substitute, chicken stock, matzos and potatoes and add to the onions and celery. Mix well. Place the mixture in a baking dish greased with nonstick spray. Bake for one hour at 350 degrees until browned.

~~

Cheese Blintzes

Serves 6

¾ cup all-purpose flour
2 tablespoons sugar
¼ teaspoon salt
¾ cup liquid egg substitute
1 cup nonfat milk
½ cup cream style cottage cheese, sieved
½ teaspoon vanilla extract
½ teaspoon cinnamon
1 cup frozen blueberries
2 tablespoons water
½ teaspoon cornstarch
1 package sugar substitute
Polyunsaturated margarine

In a mixing bowl, stir together the flour, sugar and salt. Combine ½ cup of egg substitute and milk and gradually add to the flour mixture.

Pour 2 tablespoons of the batter into a hot nonstick frying pan lightly coated with nonstick spray. Quickly swirl the batter to coat the bottom of the pan evenly and cook over medium heat until the edges begin to pull away from the pan and the bottom begins to turn golden. Loosen and turn out of the pan onto a paper towel. Repeat until all the batter has been cooked.

Stir the cottage cheese, egg substitute, vanilla extract and cinnamon together. Place a blintz leaf cooked side up and spoon 1 tablespoon of the cottage cheese mixture into the center. Fold the side into the center and roll the blintz up. Repeat with the remaining blintzes.

In a saucepan, sauté the blueberries in the water until the juice flows. Stir in the cornstarch and sugar and continue cooking until the sauce thickens.

Brown the blintzes on all sides in a small amount of polyunsaturated margarine. Serve hot topped with the blueberry sauce.

~~

Noodle Kugel

Serves 8

4 cups broad noodles, cooked and drained
¾ cup liquid egg substitute
4 tablespoons brown sugar
⅛ teaspoon nutmeg
½ cup seedless white raisins
½ cup almonds, toasted
1 tablespoon freshly squeezed lemon juice
4 tablespoons polyunsaturated margarine
2 tablespoons cornflake crumbs

Beat the egg substitute and brown sugar together until fluffy. Add the nutmeg, raisins, almonds, lemon juice and margarine. Stir in the noodles, place in a baking dish greased with nonstick spray, sprinkle with the cornflake crumbs and bake for 50 minutes at 375 degrees.

Pasta With Mussels

Serves 6

2 tablespoons extra virgin olive oil
6 anchovy fillets, chopped
3 large garlic cloves, minced
2 teaspoons dried oregano
1 teaspoon dry basil
1½ tablespoons tomato paste
2 cups diced tomatoes in juice
1 teaspoon granulated sugar
1 pound mussels, cleaned
½ pound thin spaghetti

Heat the oil in a large skillet. Add the anchovies, garlic, oregano, basil and tomato paste, stirring for 1 minute. Add the diced tomatoes and sugar and bring to a boil. Add the mussels, cover and simmer until all the shells open.

Cook the pasta in a large pot of salted water for 7 minutes until *al dente* (cooked, but firm). Drain the pasta and add to the mussels, mixing well.

~~

Quick Pasta With Tomato "Gravy"

Serves 4

1 tablespoon extra virgin olive oil
2 large shallots, sliced
2 cloves garlic, smashed
1 2-pound can San Marzano tomatoes, drained and quartered
1 teaspoon dried oregano
1 teaspoon dried basil
1 teaspoon dried rosemary
1 teaspoon kosher salt
1 teaspoon sugar
¼ cup pasta water
¼ cup parsley leaves

In a large saucepan over medium heat, cook the shallots and garlic in the oil until translucent. Add the tomatoes and bring to a boil. Add the oregano, basil and rosemary, reduce the heat to low and simmer for 10 minutes. Pour the tomatoes into a food processor and puree until smooth and thick and the tomato seeds are no longer visible. Add the salt and sugar, pulse several times and set aside.

Cook the pasta for two minutes less than the directions on the box. Drain the pasta in a colander, reserving ¼ cup of pasta water. Return the pasta to the cooking pot, add the tomatoes and pasta water, stir well and bring to a boil for 2 minutes.

Pour the pasta into a serving dish and garnish with parsley.

~~

Roasted Tomato Pizza

Serves 6

2 large beefsteak tomatoes, sliced
1 tablespoon extra virgin olive oil
1 teaspoon dried oregano
1 teaspoon dried basil
1 teaspoon dried thyme
1 teaspoon kosher salt
1 teaspoon sugar
1 pizza crust
4 ounces skim milk mozzarella
2 tablespoons Parmesan cheese, grated
2 tablespoons corn meal

Arrange the tomato slices on a cookie sheet, drizzle with the olive oil and sprinkle with the oregano, basil and thyme. Roast at 350 degrees for one hour and then cool for 15 minutes.

Place the tomatoes in a food processor, add the salt and sugar and puree until smooth and thick and no seeds are visible.

Roll the pizza crust to a 16 inch circle and place on a cookie sheet coated with corn meal. Spread the sauce over the crust. Sprinkle the cheese over the entire pizza and bake at 500 degrees for 10 minutes until the edges of the crust begin to brown and the cheese is melted.

FRAYDA FAIGEL AND HARRIS FAIGEL

Grilled Polenta

Serves 6

1 cup instant polenta
3 cups water
2 teaspoons kosher salt
2 tablespoons extra virgin olive oil
3 garlic cloves, minced
1 pound frozen spinach, defrosted and squeezed dry
¼ pound feta cheese

In a medium sauce pan, bring 3 cups of water to a boil. Add 1 teaspoon salt and whisk in the instant polenta. Cook over low heat, whisking continually for 5 minutes until the polenta is thick. Pour the hot polenta in a 9 inch square baking dish oiled with the olive oil, cover with plastic wrap and let cool for 30 minutes.

In a large skillet, heat the olive oil and sauté the garlic over medium heat for 1 minute. Increase the heat and add the spinach, stirring until it wilts.

Heat a ribbed grill pan lightly oiled with olive oil. Cut the polenta into 9 squares and grill over moderate heat until crisp and lightly charred. Place on a platter, top each piece with feta cheese and then with the warm spinach.

~~

Pasta With Roasted Sausage

Serves 4

1 quart cherry tomatoes, halved
4 tablespoons extra virgin olive oil
½ teaspoon kosher salt
¼ teaspoon freshly ground black pepper
½ teaspoon dried thyme
¼ teaspoon dried basil
4 sweet Italian sausages
1 pound thin spaghetti
½ cup grated Romano cheese
Fresh parsley

In a baking dish, combine the tomatoes, 1 tablespoon olive oil, salt, pepper, and thyme. Stir well and roast at 350 degrees for 30 minutes until the tomatoes are soft.

In a heavy skillet, heat ½ tablespoon olive oil over medium heat and brown the sausages on all sides. Drain the fat and transfer the skillet to the 350 degree oven for 15 minutes. Cool the sausages and slice into ¼ inch pieces.

Cook the spaghetti in boiling salted water for 8 minutes and drain into a colander, reserving ½ cup of pasta water.

Combine the spaghetti, remaining olive oil, roasted tomatoes and sausages, pasta water, and cheese. Garnish with parsley.

~~

Lasagna

Serves 6

1 16-ounce can diced tomatoes
1 6-ounce can tomato paste
1 teaspoon basil flakes
1 teaspoon oregano flakes
1 teaspoon rosemary
1 teaspoon sugar
1 pound low fat cottage cheese
1 pound flat non-cook lasagna noodles, uncooked
½ cup nonfat shredded mozzarella

In a saucepan, combine the diced tomatoes, tomato paste, basil, oregano, rosemary and sugar and simmer for 15 minutes to combine the flavors.

In a casserole greased with nonstick spray, place a layer of tomato sauce, then a layer of lasagna noodles, a layer of cottage cheese and then another layer of tomato sauce. Place another layer of noodles, cottage cheese and sauce and repeat until all the noodles have been used. Sprinkle the surface with the mozzarella. Bake for 45 minutes at 350 degrees.

FRAYDA FAIGEL AND HARRIS FAIGEL

Noodles a la Grecque

Serves 6

1 pound extra lean ground beef
1 6-ounce can tomato paste
6 ounces water
2 teaspoons allspice
1 teaspoon ground cinnamon
½ teaspoon nutmeg
½ teaspoon kosher salt
1 pound macaroni
1 cup grated Sapsago cheese

Sauté the meat in a nonstick pan until browned and then drain. Stir in the tomato paste, water, allspice, cinnamon, nutmeg and salt, cover and cook over low heat for 10 minutes, stirring often.

Cook the macaroni in salted water until softened, but firm. Drain. Place the macaroni in a casserole greased with nonstick spray and cover with the sauce. Sprinkle with grated cheese. Bake for 45 minutes at 350 degrees.

Cook the pasta in a large pot of salted water for 7 minutes until *al dente* (cooked, but firm). Drain the pasta and add to the mussels, mixing well.

~~

Vareniki

Serves 4

1 package Chinese dumpling leaves
1 package frozen blueberries
1 tablespoon cornstarch
¼ cup sugar
8 ounces of low fat cottage cheese
½ cup buttermilk
¼ teaspoon lemon juice
¼ teaspoon kosher salt

Combine the blueberries, cornstarch and sugar. Place one teaspoon of the filling in the center of a dumpling leaf. Run a line of water around the edges of the leaf, fold the edges together and pinch into triangular puffs. Gently seal the edges with a fork.

Combine the cottage cheese, buttermilk, lemon juice and salt in a blender. Mix well until smooth and refrigerate.

Drop the dumplings into boiling water and cook until they float and the dumpling leaf is translucent. Remove from the water with a slotted spoon, drain and serve with cottage cream sauce.

~~

Potato Kugel (2)

Serves 8

¾ cup liquid egg substitute
5 cups potato, grated and drained
½ cup potato flour
½ teaspoon baking powder
1 teaspoon kosher salt
1 onion, grated and drained
4 tablespoons polyunsaturated margarine, melted

Stir the ingredients together until smooth and mixed well. Place in a baking dish greased with nonstick spray for one hour at 350 degrees.

Chapter XVIII - Sauces

Quick Marinara Sauce

Serves 6

1 small onion, diced
3 cloves garlic, minced
2 tablespoons extra virgin olive oil
1 20-ounce can crushed tomatoes
1 6-ounce can tomato paste
1 cup dry red wine
1 teaspoon oregano
1 teaspoon basil
1 teaspoon sugar
½ teaspoon kosher salt

Sauté the onion and garlic in a skillet until translucent. Add the remaining ingredients, mix well, bring to a boil, reduce the heat and simmer for 15 minutes.

~~

Bolognese Sauce

Serves 6

1 pound ground turkey
1 medium onion, diced
1 carrot, peeled and diced
4 cloves garlic, minced
2 tablespoons polyunsaturated oil
1 20-ounce can crushed tomatoes
1 6-ounce can tomato paste
1½ teaspoons dried basil
1½ teaspoon dried oregano
½ teaspoon rosemary
1 teaspoon kosher salt
1½ teaspoons sugar

In a skillet, brown the ground turkey, breaking the meat into small pieces. Remove the meat from the pan and reserve. In the same skillet, sauté the onion, carrot and garlic in the polyunsaturated oil until softened. Add the crushed tomatoes, tomato paste, basil, oregano, rosemary, salt and sugar, mix well, bring to a boil, reduce the heat and simmer for 15 minutes. Add the browned ground turkey, mix well and simmer for 30 minutes more.

~~

Dill Cream

Serves 6

1 cup creamed cottage cheese
2 teaspoons fresh dill, finely chopped
¼ teaspoon kosher salt
⅛ teaspoon freshly ground black pepper
⅛ teaspoon lemon zest

In a covered blender at medium-high speed combine the cottage cheese, dill, salt, pepper and lemon zest until smooth and creamy. Serve as a dip or over a fresh vegetable salad or sautéed fish fillets.

~~

Creole Sauce

Serves 6

3 tablespoons polyunsaturated oil
1 small onion, diced
1 small green pepper, seeded and diced
½ cup sliced mushrooms
1 10-ounce can diced tomatoes
½ teaspoon kosher salt
¼ teaspoon freshly ground black pepper
5 drops Tabasco sauce
½ teaspoon basil

Sauté the onion, green pepper and mushrooms in the oil for 15 minutes. Add the tomatoes and seasoning and simmer for 30 minutes until the sauce thickens.

Fondue

Serves 6

2 cups low salt chicken stock
2 cups dry white wine
1 onion, diced
3 stalks celery, diced
2 garlic cloves, crushed
1 teaspoon kosher salt
½ teaspoon tarragon
1 bay leaf
½ teaspoon thyme
Lean beef or scallops

Combine all the ingredients in a saucepan and bring to a boil. Refrigerate for several days to let the flavors blend. To serve, bring the sauce back to a boil, remove the bay leaf and serve with cubed lean beef or scallops.

~~

Sweet Onion Pasta Sauce

Serves 6

2 large Vidalia onions, cut into slices and rings and separated
2 tablespoons extra virgin olive oil
1 clove garlic, minced
1 small can tomato sauce
1 small can tomato paste
½ teaspoon dried basil
½ teaspoon dried oregano
½ cup white wine
1 teaspoon sugar

Sauté the onion in the olive oil over medium heat until translucent. Add the garlic and cook until the garlic is translucent. Stir in the tomato sauce, tomato paste, basil, oregano, wine and sugar. Bring to a boil and then reduce the heat and simmer for 20 minutes.

Rosemary Sauce

Serves 6

4 large shallots, minced
2 tablespoons polyunsaturated oil
1 teaspoon freshly ground green peppercorns
1 tablespoon chopped fresh rosemary
¾ cup dry red wine
4 ounces hot water
½ teaspoon kosher salt
¼ teaspoon freshly ground black pepper

Sauté the shallots, peppercorns and rosemary in the oil until the shallots are translucent. Add the wine, bring to a boil and reduce to one-half. Serve over roasted lamb.

~~

Omelet Mushroom Sauce

Serves 6

1 pound brown mushrooms, sliced
2 tablespoons polyunsaturated margarine
1 tablespoon flour
½ cup low salt beef stock
½ teaspoon Worcestershire sauce

Sauté the mushrooms in the margarine. Blend in the flour, salt and beef stock. Add the Worcestershire, mix well, bring to a boil, reduce the heat and simmer for 5 minutes.

Omelet Tomato Sauce

Serves 6

3 tablespoons polyunsaturated margarine
1 16-ounce can diced tomatoes
2 cloves garlic, crushed
1 tablespoon chopped chives
¼ teaspoon kosher salt
⅛ teaspoon freshly ground black pepper
¼ teaspoon lemon thyme

Melt the margarine. Add the tomatoes, garlic, chives, salt, pepper and thyme and bring to a boil. Reduce the heat and simmer for 10 minutes until thickened.

~~

Pesto Genovese

Serves 6

2 large garlic cloves
¼ teaspoon kosher salt
1 cup tightly packed basil leaves
3 tablespoons pine nuts
¾ cup grated Parmesan cheese
6 tablespoons extra virgin olive oil

Puree the garlic and salt in a food processor. Add the basil in small amounts and then the pine nuts, processing into a coarse chop. Pour in the cheese and oil and continue to process until the pesto has the consistency of cream.

Chapter XIX - Bread And Muffins

Date Nut Bread

Serves 8

1 teaspoon baking soda
1 cup boiling water
½ pound dates, chopped
½ cup walnuts, toasted and chopped
½ cup polyunsaturated margarine
1 cup sugar
½ cup liquid egg substitute
2 cups all-purpose flour
1 teaspoon vanilla extract

Dissolve the baking soda in the water and pour over the dates and walnuts in a mixing bowl.

Cream the margarine, sugar and egg substitute together. Drain the dates and nuts and mix into the batter. Mix in the flour and vanilla. Pour the batter into ramekins and fill ¾ full. Bake at 350 degrees for 50 minutes until a toothpick inserted into the batter comes out clean.

Biscuits

Serves 6

2 cups sifted all-purpose flour
3 teaspoons baking powder
½ teaspoon kosher salt
¼ teaspoon polyunsaturated oil
⅔ cup nonfat milk

Preheat the oven to 475 degrees.

Sift the flour, baking powder and salt together in a mixing bowl. Mix the oil and milk together in a measuring cup and add to the flour mixture. Stir with a fork until the dough clings together. Knead the dough with the base of the hands on a floured surface about ten times. Place the dough on a 12 inch by 16 inch sheet of wax paper and pat out in a ½ inch thick layer.

Cut individual biscuits with a cookie cutter or a water glass, place on parchment paper on a cookie sheet. Bake for 12 to 15 minutes until browned.

~~

Corn Bread

Serves 6

1 cup unsifted all-purpose flour
¾ cup corn meal
2½ teaspoons baking powder
2 tablespoons sugar
⅛ teaspoon kosher salt
1 cup nonfat milk
¼ cup liquid egg substitute
¼ cup polyunsaturated oil

Grease an 8 x 8 x 2 inch pan with 1 tablespoon of the oil.

Stir the flour, corn meal, baking powder, sugar and salt together in a mixing bowl. In a separate bowl, beat the milk, egg substitute and oil together. Gradually stir the liquid into the flour and turn into the greased pan. Bake for 20 minutes at 425 degrees until golden brown. Cut into 16 squares while warm.

Chocolate Chip Walnut Banana Bread

Serves 6

1½ cups all-purpose flour
¾ cup sugar
1 teaspoon kosher salt
1 teaspoon baking soda
3 ripe bananas, mashed
½ cup liquid egg substitute
¼ cup chopped walnuts
½ cup artificial chocolate chips
½ cup white raisins

Sift together the flour, sugar, salt and baking soda.

In a mixing bowl, combine the bananas and egg substitute. Add the dry mixture, mix well and then mix in the chocolate chips and raisins. Toast the walnuts in a dry sauté pan until starting to brown and add to the batter. Bake in a nonstick 5 x 9 inch loaf pan at 350 degrees for one hour.

~~

Hushpuppies

Serves 6

1½ cups sifted cornmeal
½ cup sifted all-purpose flour
½ teaspoon kosher salt
1 teaspoon baking powder
½ teaspoon baking soda
¼ cup chopped onion
1 teaspoon sugar
1⅔ cups buttermilk
⅓ cup water
½ cup liquid egg substitute

Combine the cornmeal, flour, salt, baking powder, baking soda, onion and sugar in a mixing bowl. Add the buttermilk, water and egg substitute and stir until the batter is fully mixed. Spoon the batter onto a baking pan lined with parchment. Bake for 20 minutes at 400 degrees until browned.

Bran Muffins

Serves 6

1 cup sifted all-purpose flour
⅓ cup sugar
3 teaspoons baking powder
¾ teaspoon kosher salt
1½ cups whole bran cereal
½ stick polyunsaturated margarine, melted
1 cup nonfat milk
½ cup liquid egg substitute

Stir together the flour, sugar, baking powder and salt in a mixing bowl. Add the bran cereal.

Combine the margarine, milk and egg substitute and add to the flour mixture stirring quickly until the dry ingredients are moistened and the batter is lumpy. Divide the batter into 12 muffin cups. Bake for 25 minutes at 400 degrees until done.

~~

Blueberry Muffins

Serves 6

2 cups sifted all-purpose flour
⅓ cup sugar
3 teaspoons baking powder
¾ teaspoon kosher salt
½ stick polyunsaturated margarine
¾ cup nonfat milk
1 cup fresh or frozen blueberries
¼ cup liquid egg substitute

Mix the flour, sugar, baking powder and salt. Cut in the cold margarine until mixed. Combine the milk, blueberries and egg substitute and add to the flour mixture. Stir until the dry ingredients are moist and lumpy. Divide the batter into 12 muffin cups. Bake for 20 minutes at 425 degrees until browned on top.

Chapter XX - Desserts

Pineapple Cranberry Sorbet

Serves 6

1 cup crushed pineapple
1 cup whole cranberry sauce
1 teaspoon unflavored gelatin
¼ cup cold water
2 tablespoons freshly squeezed lemon juice
1 teaspoon fresh lemon zest

In a saucepan, cook the pineapple, cranberry sauce and
sugar until the sugar is dissolved. Soften the gelatin in the
cold water and add to the fruit mixture. Stir in the lemon
juice and zest, pour into a shallow baking dish and freeze for
3 hours, stirring occasionally.

~~

Blackberry Crisp

Serves 4

½ stick polyunsaturated margarine
⅓ cup unsifted all-purpose flour
⅓ cup brown sugar
¾ cups rolled oats
1 quart fresh blackberries
⅓ cup sugar

Mix the margarine, flour, sugar and oats until blended.
Place the blackberries in an 8-inch square baking dish and
sprinkle with the sugar and flour mixture. Bake for 30
minutes at 350 degrees until lightly browned.

Blueberry Pineapple Trifle

Serves 6

4 cups stale white cake, cut into 1-inch cubes
1½ sticks polyunsaturated margarine
¼ cup sugar
1 teaspoon allspice
1 cup fresh pineapple, cut into ½ inch cubes
2 cups fresh or frozen blueberries
2 teaspoons freshly squeezed lemon juice
1 teaspoon fresh lemon zest
½ cup brown sugar

Combine the cake cubes, margarine, sugar and spice and mix well.

Sprinkle the pineapple and berries with lemon juice, zest and brown sugar. Alternate layers of cake mixture and pineapple-berry mixture in an 8-inch square baking dish greased with nonstick spray. Bake for 20 minutes at 350 degrees until bubbly. Serve warm or cold.

~~

Angel Food Cake

Serves 8

1½ cups sifted cake flour
½ cup sugar, not sifted
1½ cups egg whites
1 teaspoon vanilla extract
1 tablespoon freshly squeezed lemon juice
1¼ teaspoons cream of tartar
¼ teaspoon kosher salt
1⅓ cups sifted sugar
1½ cups sifted confectioners sugar
3 tablespoons lemonade
½ teaspoon fresh lemon zest

Add unsifted sugar to the sifted flour, sift again 4 times and reserve.

Combine the egg whites, cream of tartar, salt and beat to soft peaks.

In a separate bowl, mix the vanilla and lemon juice. Add the rest of the sugar in four parts, mixing well between each until well blended. Sift in the flour mixture in four parts.

Fold in the egg whites with a large spoon.

Bake in a 10-inch tube cake pan for 30 to 40 minutes at 375 degrees. Remove from the oven, invert and cool on a wire rack.

Mix the confectioners sugar, lemonade and lemon zest together to frost the cake.

~~

Pie Crust (1)

Serves 8

1 cup sifted all-purpose flour
1 tablespoon sugar
½ teaspoon kosher salt
1 teaspoon baking powder
¼ pound polyunsaturated margarine
Ice cold water

Sift the flour, sugar, salt and baking powder together into a bowl. Blend in the margarine and mix until the margarine dissolves. You may need a teaspoonful of the ice water to get the dough to rolling consistency.

Shape the dough into a ball, place it between 2 sheets of waxed paper and roll out with a rolling pin. Remove the top layer of waxed paper, invert the dough over a pie plate and remove the paper. Fit the dough to the plate and trim the edges. Flute the margins with a fork.

If the dough is to be baked now, prick the bottom with a fork and bake for 10 minutes at 400 degrees. Cool before filling.

If the dough will be baked with a filling, do not prick the bottom

For a 2-crust pie, make a second crust recipe.

Pie Crust (2)

Serves 8

1 cup sifted all-purpose flour
¾ teaspoon kosher salt
¾ teaspoon sugar
¼ cup polyunsaturated oil
2 tablespoons cold nonfat milk

Mix the flour, sugar and salt in a bowl. Combine the oil and milk in a measuring cup, pour quickly into the flour mixture and stir well until blended into a ball.

Shape the dough into a ball, place between two sheets of waxed paper and roll out with a rolling pin. Remove the top layer of waxed paper, invert the dough over a pie plate and remove the paper. Fit the dough to the pan, trim the edges and flute the rim with a fork.

If the dough is baked now, prick the bottom with a fork and bake for 10 minutes at 400 degrees. Cool before filling.

If the dough will be baked with a filling, do not prick the bottom.

For a 2-crust pie, make a second crust recipe.

~~

Oatmeal Raisin Chocolate Chip Cookies

Serves 8

2 cups sifted all-purpose flour
1¼ cups sugar
1 teaspoon baking powder
½ teaspoon kosher salt
1 teaspoon cinnamon
3 cups rolled oats
1 cup white raisins
¼ cup chocolate chips
¼ cup walnuts, toasted and chopped
¼ cup pecans, toasted and chopped
1 cup polyunsaturated oil
½ cup liquid egg substitute
½ cup freshly squeezed orange juice
1 teaspoon fresh orange zest

Stir together the flour, sugar, baking powder and salt. Add the oats, raisins, nuts and chocolate chips and stir well. Add the oil, egg substitute, orange juice and zest and mix until well blended.

Drop the dough by the teaspoonful 1½ inches apart on a cookie sheet covered with parchment paper.

Bake for 10-12 minutes at 400 degrees until lightly browned. Remove with a spatula and cool on a wire rack.

~~

Chocolate Cake

Serves 12

2 cups unsifted cake flour
½ cup cocoa powder
3½ teaspoons baking powder
1 teaspoon kosher salt
¾ cup polyunsaturated margarine
1½ cup sugar
1 teaspoon vanilla extract
¾ cup liquid egg substitute
1 cup nonfat milk

Sift together the flour, cocoa, baking powder and salt and set aside.

Beat the margarine and sugar until the mixture is light and fluffy. Beat in the vanilla extract. Gradually add the egg substitute. Add half the dry ingredients and then half the milk, followed by the rest of the dry ingredients and the remaining milk, beating well after each addition.

Grease two 8-inch round cake pans with nonstick spray and then flour each lightly. Pour half the batter into each pan. Bake at 350 degrees for 30 minutes or until a toothpick can be removed free of batter. Cool in the pans for 10 minutes and then turn out onto a wire rack for finish. Frost when completely cool.

Fruit Compote

Serves 6

1 16-ounce can apricot halves
1 16-ounce can plums, pitted and halved
1 16-ounce can peach halves
1 teaspoon fresh lemon zest
2 tablespoons polyunsaturated margarine
2 tablespoons brown sugar
⅓ cup freshly squeezed orange juice
1 tablespoon cornstarch
¼ teaspoon cinnamon
¼ teaspoon fresh nutmeg
1 teaspoon Curacao

Arrange the fruit in a baking dish coated with the margarine. Sprinkle with the spices and Curacao.

In a saucepan, melt the margarine and stir in the brown sugar. Mix the cornstarch and orange juice, add to the margarine and heat until thickened. Drizzle over the fruit.

Bake for 20 minutes at 350 degrees.

Serve warm, cold or as a topping on cake.

~~

Fruit Cobbler

Serves 6

2 cups of fruit (blueberries, cherries, raspberries, blackberries or a mixture).
⅓ cup sugar
¼ teaspoon cinnamon
1 cup sifted all-purpose flour
1 teaspoon baking powder
1 teaspoon kosher salt
⅔ cup sugar
¼ cup polyunsaturated margarine
¾ cup nonfat milk
½ teaspoon vanilla extract

Combine the fruit, ⅓ cup sugar and cinnamon and spread in an 8-inch baking dish greased with nonstick spray. Combine the flour, baking powder, salt and ⅔ cups sugar in another bowl. Mix the margarine, milk and vanilla in a blender for one minute. Pour the liquid over the dry ingredients and mix well. Pour the batter over the berries and stir together.

Bake for 35 minutes at 350 degrees. Serve warm or cold.

~~

White Cake

Serves 12

2 cups sifted cake flour
1 teaspoon kosher salt
1½ cups sugar
½ cup polyunsaturated oil
1 cup nonfat milk
3 teaspoons baking powder
4 egg whites
1 teaspoon vanilla extract

Sift together in a mixing bowl the flour, salt and sugar. Add the oil and ⅔ cup milk. Stir until the flour is damp and beat for 1 minute. Stir in the baking powder and then add the remaining milk, the egg whites and vanilla extract. Beat for two minutes.

Grease one 10-inch tube pan or two 8-inch round cake pans with non stick spray and dust with flour. Pour half the batter into each round pan or all of the batter into the tube pan. Bake at 350 degrees for 35 minutes or until a toothpick can be removed free of batter. Cool in the pan for 10 minutes and then turn out onto a wire rack to complete cooling. Dust with confectioner's sugar or frost when completely cool.

Strawberry Mousse

Serves 6

1 16-ounce package frozen strawberries, thawed, juice reserved.
½ cup non fat dry milk powder
1 egg white, stiffly beaten
2 tablespoons freshly squeezed lemon juice
4 tablespoons sugar

Beat the milk powder and strawberry juice until soft peaks form. Add the lemon juice and continue to beat until the peaks are firm. Gradually stir in half the sugar.

In a separate bowl, mash the strawberries and mix with the rest of the sugar. Fold the whipped milk and mashed berries into the beaten egg white, pour into parfait glasses and freeze.

~~

Walnut Sugar Cookies

Serves 8

1 cup polyunsaturated margarine
¾ cup sugar
¼ cup liquid egg substitute
1 tablespoon fresh lemon zest
2⅓ cups unsifted all-purpose flour
2 teaspoons baking powder
½ cup walnuts, toasted and chopped
¼ cup sugar

Cream together the margarine and ¾ cup sugar. Add the egg substitute and lemon zest.

In a separate bowl, blend the flour and baking powder, stir into the margarine and mix well.

Drop the batter 2 inches apart by the tablespoonful onto a cookie sheet covered with parchment paper and flatten with the bottom of a water glass.

Bake for 8 to 10 minutes at 375 degrees until the edges are lightly browned. Sprinkle with the sugar, remove from the cookie sheet with a spatula and place on a wire rack to cool.

Chocolate Sandies

Serves 8

¾ cup polyunsaturated margarine
⅓ cup sugar
3 tablespoons water
1 teaspoon vanilla extract
1¾ cups all-purpose flour
½ cup pecans, toasted and chopped
½ cup artificial chocolate bits

Cream the margarine and sugar until fluffy. Beat in the water and vanilla extract. Blend in the flour, then the pecans and chocolate bits.

Shape the dough into 1-inch balls using 2 teaspoons, place on a cookie sheet covered with parchment paper and flatten slightly with the base of the hand.

Bake at 350 degrees for 20 minutes, remove with a spatula to a wire rack to cool.

~~

Apple Pie

Serves 8

1 cup sugar
1½ teaspoons fresh ground cinnamon
6 cups sliced apples
1 tablespoon liquid egg substitute

In a bowl, mix the sugar, cinnamon and apples.

Prepare a double recipe of one of the unbaked pie crusts and line a 9-inch pie plate with one of them. Fill the pie plate with the apples and cover with the second crust. Fit the second crust to the plate, trim the edges and seal the layers together with a fork. Brush the top with the egg substitute and pierce the top of the pie with a knife several times.

Bake for 45 minutes at 425 degrees until the top is browned and the apples are soft.

Pear Cobbler

Serves 8

8 ripe pears, cored and cut into ¼ inch slices
1½ tablespoons fresh ginger, grated
½ cup plus 3 tablespoons sugar
Zest of one lemon
Juice of one lemon
2 cups flour
½ teaspoon household salt
1 tablespoon baking powder
2 tablespoons polyunsaturated margarine
½ cup liquid egg substitute
⅓ cup nonfat milk
1 cup chopped walnuts and pecans

Combine the pears, ginger, ½ cup sugar, lemon zest and juice and place in a casserole dish. In a second bowl, combine the flour, salt, baking powder and 1 tablespoon of sugar and combine with the margarine into a crumbly mixture. Beat the milk and egg substitute together and add to the mixture. Dot the pears with dough, flatten slightly and sprinkle with the remaining sugar and the chopped nuts. Bake at 425 degrees for 40 minutes until brown.

~~

Chocolate Rum Wafers

Serves 8

1½ cups sifted all-purpose flour
¾ cups cocoa powder
1¼ teaspoons baking powder
⅛ teaspoon kosher salt
1¼ cups sugar
¾ cup polyunsaturated margarine
1 tablespoon dark rum
¼ cup liquid egg substitute

Sift together the flour, cocoa powder, baking powder and salt and set aside.

Blend the sugar and margarine and beat in the rum and egg substitute. Stir in the flour mixture and mix well. Form the dough into a ball, wrap in clear plastic wrap and chill in the refrigerator for one hour.

Roll the dough on a lightly floured board to ⅛ inch thickness. Cut the cookies with a cookie cutter and place on a cookie sheet covered with parchment paper.

Bake for 8 minutes at 400 degrees, remove with a spatula and cool on a wire rack.

~~

Flourless Brownies

Serves 8

½ cup liquid egg substitute
1 cup sugar
5½ tablespoons cocoa powder
½ cup polyunsaturated oil
½ cup cake meal
¼ teaspoon kosher salt
½ cup walnuts, toasted and chopped

Beat the egg substitute and sugar together. Add the oil and then mix in the cocoa powder, cake meal, salt and nuts. Pour into a shallow pan greased with nonfat spray.

Bake for 20 to 30 minutes at 350 degrees until a toothpick is clean when removed.

~~

Graham Cracker Crust

Serves 8

1½ cups graham cracker crumbs
¼ cup sugar
¼ cup polyunsaturated margarine, melted

Combine the graham cracker crumbs, sugar and melted margarine. Press firmly against the bottom and sides of a 9-inch pie plate.

Bake for 10 minutes at 350 degrees. Cool before filling.

Flourless Banana Cake

Serves 10

1½ cups liquid egg substitute
1 cup sugar
¾ cups cake meal
¼ cup potato starch
Juice and zest of one lemon
2 ripe bananas, mashed
¼ cup polyunsaturated oil
½ cup walnuts, toasted and finely chopped

Mix the egg substitute and sugar and reserve.

Mix the cake meal and cornstarch and make a well in the middle. Add the oil, lemon juice, zest and bananas and fold in. Pour into a baking pan greased with nonstick spray. Bake for one hour at 325 degrees. Remove from the oven, invert the pan and cool on a wire rack.

~~

Honey Cake

Serves 12

¼ cup liquid egg substitute
1 cup sugar
3¼ cups all-purpose flour
2 teaspoons baking powder
1 teaspoon baking soda
1 teaspoon ground dried ginger
1 teaspoon cinnamon
1 teaspoon freshly ground nutmeg
1 cup honey
1 cup boiled coffee
2 tablespoons polyunsaturated oil
2 tablespoons chopped toasted walnuts

Slowly beat the egg substitute and sugar together.

In another bowl, stir the dry ingredients together, add the coffee, honey and oil and add to the egg mixture.

Grease a 5 x 9 inch pan with non stick spray, sprinkle with the walnuts. Pour in the batter. Bake at 350 degrees for 40 minutes. Cool in the pan for 10 minutes, turn onto a wire rack and finish cooling.

Cherry Pie

Serves 8

1 9-inch pie crust using recipe 1 or 2 (above)
2 16-ounce cans pitted sour cherries
1 cup sugar
3 tablespoons quick-cooking tapioca
⅛ teaspoon kosher salt
½ teaspoon almond extract

Drain the cherries, reserving ⅔ cup of the liquid. Combine the cherries, sugar, tapioca, salt, reserved juice, salt and almond extract and stir.

Fill the pie crust. Bake for 35 minutes at 425 degrees, then reduce the heat to 350 and bake for 35 minutes more.

~~

Mandarin Orange Cheesecake

Serves 12

¾ cups graham cracker crumbs
3 tablespoons plus ¼ cup sugar
¼ stick polyunsaturated margarine, melted
1 tablespoon polyunsaturated oil
1 3-ounce package orange gelatin
1 cup boiling water
1 tablespoon orange zest
1½ pound low fat cottage cheese

1 11-ounce can mandarin oranges, drained
½ cup orange marmalade

Combine the graham crackers, 3 tablespoons sugar, margarine and oil and press into a spring-form pan.

In a medium saucepan, stir the gelatin into the boiling water until dissolved. Add the orange zest and cool.

Drain the mandarin oranges and arrange on top of the cake. Warm the marmalade and brush over the top of the cake. Chill for one hour before unmolding and serving.

Apple Cake

Serves 10

⅓ cup softened polyunsaturated margarine
¾ cup sugar
½ cup liquid egg substitute
½ teaspoon vanilla
1⅓ cups unsifted flour
½ cup nonfat milk
2½ teaspoons baking powder
¼ teaspoon household salt
1 teaspoon ground cinnamon
¼ cup raisins
4 cups peeled, sliced apples brushed with lemon juice
¼ cup brown sugar

Blend the margarine and sugar until creamy. Beat in the egg and vanilla. Alternate adding the flour and the milk. Add the baking powder and salt. Fold in the raisins and pour the mixture into an 8 inch square pan greased with nonstick spray. Arrange the apples on top of the batter, sprinkle with cinnamon and brown sugar. Bake at 375 degrees for 1 hour. Serve warm.

~~

Apple Crumb Pudding

Serves 4

1½ cups graham cracker crumbs
½ stick polyunsaturated margarine, melted
½ teaspoon freshly ground nutmeg
2 teaspoons cinnamon
½ cup chopped toasted pecans
½ cup raisins
2 cups applesauce
1½ teaspoons freshly squeezed lemon juice
¼ teaspoon lemon zest

Combine the graham cracker crumbs and melted margarine with nutmeg, cinnamon, pecans and raisins. Put ⅓ of the mixture in a 1½ quart casserole sprayed with nonstick spray.

Combine the applesauce, lemon juice and zest and pour ⅓ into the casserole. Cover with ⅓ of the crumbs and the remaining applesauce mixture. Cover with the remaining crumbs. Bake for 25 minutes at 350 degrees until lightly browned. Serve warm or chilled.

~~

Pineapple Chiffon Pie

Serves 8

1 3-ounce package lemon gelatin
1 cup boiling water
1 cup crushed pineapple
2 tablespoons freshly squeezed lemon juice
⅓ cup nonfat dry milk powder
1 baked 9-inch graham cracker crust

Dissolve the gelatin in the boiling water. Drain the pineapple and reserve the juice. Add the lemon juice and enough water to the pineapple juice to make 1 cup, add to the gelatin and chill until jelled.

Sprinkle the milk powder over the gelatin and beat with an electric mixer until the volume doubles. Fold into the pie shell and refrigerate for one hour before serving.

~~

Blueberry Pie

Serves 8

2 quarts fresh blueberries
1 cup sugar
3 tablespoons cornstarch
2 9-inch pie crusts, (double recipe)
1 tablespoon liquid egg substitute

Mix the blueberries, sugar and cornstarch together. Pour the berries into the pie plate and cover with the second crust. Trim the second crust and seal the edges with a fork. Brush the top with the liquid egg substitute.

Bake for 35 minutes at 350 degrees until the crust is lightly browned. Cool on a wire rack before serving.

Pumpkin Pie

Serves 8

1 12-ounce can (2 cups) pumpkin
1 16-ounce can sweetened condensed milk
1 cup liquid egg substitute
1 teaspoon ground cinnamon
½ teaspoon ginger powder
½ teaspoon nutmeg
½ teaspoon household salt
1 9-inch unbaked pie shell

Combine the pumpkin, condensed milk, egg substitute, cinnamon, ginger, nutmeg and salt and place in the pie shell. Bake for 15 minutes at 425 degrees. Then reduce the temperature to 350 degrees and bake for 35 minutes until a knife inserted 1 inch from the edge comes out clean.

~~

Pecan Squares

Serves 12

¼ pound polyunsaturated margarine
3 cups light brown sugar
½ cup liquid egg substitute
2 cups all-purpose flour
1 teaspoon vanilla extract
½ teaspoon kosher salt
½ cup pecans, toasted and coarsely chopped

Mix the margarine, 2 cups brown sugar, egg substitute, flour, vanilla and salt and beat until smooth. Spread the batter over a shallow baking pan lined with parchment paper.

Spread ¼ cup liquid egg substitute over the batter. Sprinkle ½ cup light brown sugar and pecans. Then spread the remaining brown sugar over the top.

Bake for 20 minutes at 350 degrees. Cut into squares and cool.

Chocolate Buttermilk Cake

Serves 12

1⅔ cup all-purpose flour
1 cup sugar
½ cup cocoa powder
1 teaspoon kosher salt
1 cup buttermilk
½ cup polyunsaturated oil
1½ teaspoons vanilla extract

Sift together the flour, sugar, cocoa powder and salt. Beat in the buttermilk, oil and vanilla until smooth.

Grease a 9 x 12 inch baking pan with nonstick spray. Pour the batter into the pan. Bake at 375 degrees for 30 minutes or until a toothpick can be removed free of batter. Cool in the pan for 10 minutes and turn onto a wire rack to finish cooling. Dust with confectioner's sugar or frost when fully cooled.

~~

Strawberry Pie

Serves 8

1 quart fresh strawberries
1 cup sugar
3 tablespoons cornstarch
1 tablespoon polyunsaturated margarine
1 9-inch graham cracker pie crust

Wash and hull the strawberries and drain thoroughly. Crush 2 cups of berries and add enough water to make 2 cups of liquid. Combine the crushed berries, sugar and cornstarch and cook over low heat, stirring constantly, until thickened. Slice the remaining berries and add to the mixture, cooking for one minute more. Add the margarine and cool. Pour the berry mix into the pie crust and refrigerate for 2 hours before serving.

Lemon Crisps

Serves 8

⅔ cup polyunsaturated margarine
½ cup firmly packed brown sugar
1 teaspoon freshly squeezed lemon juice
1 teaspoon fresh lemon zest
⅔ cup sifted all-purpose flour
1½ cups rolled oats

Cream the margarine and sugar. Add the lemon juice and zest, flour, oats and mix until blended well. Form the dough into small balls and place on a cookie sheet covered with parchment paper and flatten with a fork.

Bake for 13 to 15 minutes at 325 degrees until lightly browned. Remove with a spatula and cool on a wire rack.

~~

Frozen Banana Mousse

Serves 6

3 cups mashed bananas
⅔ cup sugar
⅛ teaspoon kosher salt
½ cup pineapple juice
1 tablespoon fresh squeezed lemon juice
1 teaspoon fresh orange zest
2 tablespoons Cointreau
1 teaspoon powdered ginger
2 egg whites, beaten stiff

Mix all the ingredients but the egg whites and fold into the egg whites. Fill parfait glasses and freeze.

~~

Cornflake Walnut Crust

Serves 8

1½ cups cornflakes, crushed
¼ cup sugar
1¼ sticks polyunsaturated margarine, melted
¾ teaspoon cinnamon
½ cup walnuts, toasted and finely chopped

Combine all the ingredients in a 9-inch pie plate, mix well and press against the sides and bottom.

Bake for 10 minutes at 350 degrees. Cool before filling.

Pecan Pie

Serves 8

¾ cup liquid egg substitute
½ cup sugar
1 cup dark corn syrup
¼ teaspoon kosher salt
¼ cup polyunsaturated margarine, melted
1 cup pecans, toasted and chopped
1 teaspoon vanilla extract
1 9-inch pie crust

Beat the egg substitute and add the sugar, corn syrup, salt, margarine, pecans and vanilla extract. Pour the batter into the pie crust.

Bake for 10 minutes at 450 degrees. Reduce the heat to 300 degrees and bake for 35 minutes more. Cool on a wire rack.

Chapter XXI - Frostings

Whipped "Cream"

½ teaspoon unflavored gelatin
6 tablespoons nonfat milk
½ cup ice water
½ cup nonfat dry milk powder
¾ teaspoon vanilla extract
1¼ tablespoons granulated sugar

Chill a bowl in the refrigerator.

Soften the gelatin in 1 tablespoon of nonfat milk. Heat the remaining milk and add the softened gelatin, stirring until dissolved and set aside to thicken.

Pour the ice water into the chilled bowl, add 2 tablespoons of nonfat dry milk powder and beat for one minute at high speed. Reduce the speed to low and add the remaining milk powder. At medium speed, add the sugar and vanilla. Increase to high speed, add the gelatin mixture and beat for 10 minutes. Refrigerate for 3 hours before serving.

~~

Chocolate Frosting

6 tablespoons cocoa powder
1 cup confectioners sugar
1 tablespoon polyunsaturated margarine
Boiling water

Mix cocoa powder, sugar and margarine. Add boiling water one teaspoon at a time until the frosting reaches spreading consistency.

Chocolate Boiled Frosting

¼ cup cocoa powder
2 tablespoons cornstarch
¾ cup sugar
⅛ teaspoon kosher salt
1 cup nonfat milk
½ teaspoon polyunsaturated margarine
1 teaspoon vanilla extract

Sift together the cocoa powder, cornstarch, sugar and salt. Add the milk and cook over low-to-medium heat, stirring constantly until thick. Remove from the heat and blend in the margarine and vanilla. Cool to room temperature before spreading.

~~

Lemon Frosting

1¼ cup sugar
⅓ cup water
2 egg whites
⅓ teaspoon cream of tartar
½ teaspoon vanilla extract
1 tablespoon freshly squeezed lemon juice
1 teaspoon fresh lemon zest

Boil the sugar and water until the syrup spins threads when dropped from the back of a spoon.

Beat the egg whites until foamy, add the cream of tartar and continue beating until stiff. Slowly add the syrup beating constantly until the frosting holds its shape. Stir in the vanilla, lemon juice and lemon zest. Cool to room temperature before spreading.

FRAYDA FAIGEL AND HARRIS FAIGEL

Vanilla Frosting

1 egg white
¼ cup sugar
¼ teaspoon cream of tartar
1 teaspoon vanilla extract
¼ cup water

Combine the ingredients in the top of a double boiler, set over hot water in the bottom of the double boiler and beat until the mixture stands in stiff peaks.

This frosting may be colored with vegetable coloring.

Chapter XXII - Breakfast

Pancakes

Serves 4

¼ **cup liquid egg substitute**
1½ **cups nonfat milk**
2 **tablespoons polyunsaturated margarine, melted**
1½ **cups sifted all-purpose flour**
2 **tablespoons sugar**
1½ **teaspoons baking powder**
1 **teaspoon kosher salt**
½ **teaspoon baking soda**
Sliced banana, blueberries, or artificial chocolate chips (optional)

Mix together the egg substitute, nonfat milk and melted margarine.

Combine the flour, sugar, baking powder, salt and baking soda. Add the liquid ingredients to the dry ingredients and beat until the dry ingredients are moistened and the batter is wet and lumpy.

Pour onto a hot griddle one large tablespoon at a time for each pancake. Cook until the pancakes are puffed and bubbly. Turn with a spatula and continue cooking until the underside is browned.

Sliced bananas or blueberries or artificial chocolate chips can be added to the batter before cooking.

French Toast

Serves 2

1 cup liquid egg substitute
¼ cup nonfat milk
1 teaspoon vanilla
4 slices 2 day old challah bread,
1 tablespoon polyunsaturated margarine

Mix the egg substitute, milk and vanilla in a large bowl. Soak the stale bread slices in the mixture, preferably overnight.

In a skillet, melt the margarine and sauté the soaked bread until the bottom is turning brown. Turn the bread over and continue to sauté until the new bottom is also brown.

~~

Omelet

Serves 2

1 cup liquid egg substitute
¼ teaspoon kosher salt
½ teaspoon cream of tartar
2 teaspoons polyunsaturated oil
¼ green pepper, diced
¼ onion, diced
4 mushrooms, sliced
4 cherry tomatoes, quartered
1 teaspoon Canadian bacon, diced (optional)
1 ounce part-skim mozzarella or Sapsago cheese, grated

Combine the egg substitute, salt and cream of tartar in a bowl and beat until blended and frothy.

Heat an omelet pan or 8-inch skillet. Add the oil and heat. Pour in the egg mixture and cook undisturbed until the bottom is set and the top begins to become firm. Loosen the eggs with a spatula. Sprinkle the vegetables and cheese (and optional Canadian bacon) over the entire surface and fold the omelet in half. Reduce the heat and cook covered for 10 minutes.

Frittata

Serves 2

1 tablespoon polyunsaturated oil
½ small white onion, sliced
¼ green pepper, sliced
2 large brown mushrooms, sliced
¼ cup liquid egg substitute
1 large egg, beaten
¼ teaspoon salt
1 small tomato, sliced
½ cup low fat cottage cheese
1 tablespoon grated Romano cheese

Sauté the onion, pepper and mushrooms in the oil in a skillet until the onion is translucent.

Mix the egg substitute, egg and salt together until blended and pour over the vegetables and cook until the eggs are beginning to firm. Spread the cottage cheese over the eggs, then a layer of tomato slices and then a sprinkling of Romano cheese. Cover the skillet and continue cooking until the frittata is firm. Slide the frittata onto a serving dish and allow it to cool for several minutes before cutting.

Chapter XXIII - Sandwiches

Toasted Chicken

Serves 4

8 slices potato bread
4 teaspoons plus 3 tablespoons polyunsaturated margarine
2 cups sliced cooked chicken breast
8 slices tomato
½ teaspoon kosher salt
1 cup liquid egg substitute

Spread 4 slices of bread with the 4 teaspoons margarine. Top with the chicken slices and tomato slices. Sprinkle with salt and top with the remaining 4 slices of bread.

Dip the sandwiches in the egg substitute, coating evenly. Grill in a sauté pan in the remaining margarine over medium heat until the bottom begins to brown. Turn and continue grilling until the new bottom begins to brown. Cut into triangles. Serve hot.

~~

Sloppy Joe

Serves 8

1 pound extra lean ground chuck
½ cup chopped celery
½ cup chopped green pepper
½ cup chopped onion
2 cups crushed tomatoes
½ teaspoon basil
½ teaspoon oregano
1 teaspoon sugar
½ teaspoon kosher salt
¼ teaspoon chili powder
½ teaspoon Tabasco sauce
1 cup salted peanuts (optional)
8 hamburger buns, split and toasted

Brown the beef in a large nonstick skillet, crumbling the meat with a fork. Drain the fat. Add the celery, green pepper, onion, crushed tomatoes, basil, oregano, sugar, salt, chili powder and Tabasco and stir well. Cover and simmer for 20 minutes, stirring occasionally.

If using the peanuts, stir in just before serving.

Fill each bun with ½ cup of the meat mixture.

~~

Meatloaf Sandwich

Serves 4

4 loaves Pita bread
8 ounces meat loaf
½ teaspoon oregano
1 teaspoon mint
1 medium tomato, diced
2 tablespoons polyunsaturated oil
2 tablespoons freshly squeezed lemon juice
4 lettuce leaves

Crumble the meatloaf in a mixing bowl and add the oregano, mint, tomato, oil and lemon juice. Mix thoroughly.

Carefully remove the tip of each Pita loaf, spread the side open, insert a lettuce leaf and then stuff each one with ¼ of the meat mixture.

~~

Westerner

Serves 4

3 ounces dry extra lean corned beef, diced
¼ teaspoon kosher salt
2 cups liquid egg substitute
2 tablespoons polyunsaturated oil
4 hard rolls, toasted

Mix the diced beef, salt and egg substitute and cook slowly in the oil. Serve in the hard rolls.

Club Sandwich

Serves 4

4 ounces sliced roasted chicken breast
2 ounces sliced extra lean pastrami
3 ounces extra lean corned beef
1 cup fresh mushrooms, sliced
1 medium green pepper, cut into rings
4 onion rolls, toasted
Thousand Island or Russian dressing
Cherry tomatoes
Sweet gherkins

On each roll, place one ounce of chicken, ½ ounce of pastrami and ¼ of the corned beef. Top with the pepper rings and fill the opening with mushrooms. Spread each with Thousand Island or Russian dressing and garnish with cherry tomatoes and sweet gherkins.

~~

Corned Beef Omelet Sandwich

Serves 4

3 ounces extra lean corned beef
2 cups liquid egg substitute
¼ teaspoon cream of tartar
½ cup diced sweet red pepper
½ cup fresh mushrooms, sliced
4 seeded sandwich or bulky rolls, toasted
2 tablespoon polyunsaturated oil
Cherry tomatoes

Whisk the egg substitute and cream of tartar together until frothy. Fold in the corned beef, red pepper and mushrooms and cook in the oil in a skillet until firm.

Serve on seeded or bulky rolls garnished with cherry tomatoes.

Tunakraut

Serves 4

1 5-ounce can tuna, packed in water, drained
⅓ cup mayonnaise
4 tablespoons grated Sapsago cheese
½ cup sauerkraut
4 hard rolls, split

Flake the tuna in a bowl, blend in the mayonnaise and spread on the bottom half of each roll. Top each with sauerkraut and 1 tablespoon cheese. Cover each with the top of the roll and bake for 5 minutes at 350 degrees until toasted.

~~

Summer Garden Sandwich

Serves 2

2 large tomatoes, cored and thinly sliced
4 large lettuce leaves
2 thin slices red onion
8 thin cucumber slices
2 potato rolls
6 teaspoons mayonnaise
4 gherkins

Toast the potato rolls. Spread the bottom half of each roll with 2 teaspoons of mayonnaise. Place a layer of lettuce, then cucumber, then tomato and finally onion on the bottom of each roll. Spread the top of each roll with 1 teaspoon of mayonnaise.

Garnish with the gherkins

Recipe Index

THE HAPPY HEART COOKBOOK

Rosstrum Publishing issues a variety of books. Currently available are the following:

Fiction:
Lawless in Brazil, by Mike Johnson
Timberline, by Bernie Ziegner
Pursuit, by Bernie Ziegner
A Shadow on the Wall, by Dale T. Phillips

Non-Fiction:
Fast Track for Caregivers, by Esther and Joseph Ross
366 Tips for a Successful Job Search, by Cynthia Wright
How to Improve Your Interviewing Skills, by Dale T. Phillips
The Dave Maynard Spin, by Dave Maynard and Suzan Franks
Journey of a Beam, by Christina Green

Poetry:
Emotions in Motion, by Peggy L'Ecuyer

For information on these and other forthcoming works,
Go to
www.rosstrumpublishing.com

www.ingramcontent.com/pod-product-compliance
Lightning Source LLC
Chambersburg PA
CBHW060746100426
42813CB00032B/3416/J